WARRIOR • 139

BYZANTINE CAVALRYMAN
c.900–1204

TIMOTHY DAWSON

ILLUSTRATED BY GIUSEPPE RAVA
Series editors Marcus Cowper and Nikolai Bogdanovic

First published in Great Britain in 2009 by Osprey Publishing
Midland House, West Way, Botley, Oxford, OX2 0PH, UK
44-02 23rd St, Suite 219, Long Island City, NY 11101, USA
Email: info@ospreypublishing.com

© 2009 Osprey Publishing Ltd.

A CIP catalogue record for this book is available from the British Library.

ISBN: 978 1 84603 404 6
e-Book ISBN: 978 1 84908 090 3

Editorial by Ilios Publishing Ltd, Oxford, UK (www.iliospublishing.com)
Page layout by Mark Holt
Index by Alison Worthington
Typeset in Sabon and Myriad Pro
Originated by PPS Grasmere
Printed in China through Worldprint Ltd

10 11 12 13 14   11 10 9 8 7 6 5 4 3 2

ACKNOWLEDGEMENTS

The author wishes to thank the following people for their considerable assistance: Debs Crossley, David Wiray of the Northern Equestrian Centre, Dewsbury, Alan Larsen and the long-suffering and hard-working ladies of the Festival of History equestrian ground crew, and Steven Baker, a long-suffering friend.

ARTIST'S NOTE

Readers may care to note that the original paintings from which the colour plates in this book were prepared are available for private sale. The Publishers retain all reproduction copyright whatsoever. All enquiries should be addressed to:

Giuseppe Rava
via the following website:
www.g-rava.it.

The Publishers regret that they can enter into no correspondence upon this matter.

THE WOODLAND TRUST

Osprey Publishing are supporting the Woodland Trust, the UK's leading woodland conservation charity, by funding the dedication of trees.

CONTENTS

BYZANTINE CAVALRYMAN
c. 900–1204

INTRODUCTION

Consult a dictionary and under 'Byzantine' you will find it described as an adjective meaning something like 'complex, inflexible or underhand'. What should we make, therefore, of the suggestion that there was such a thing as the 'Byzantine Empire'. The answer to that lies in where and by whom the term originated. It first appears in print in 1557 from the pen of a German, Hieronymus Wolf. In the tenth century Germany had looked to Byzantium (medieval Greek Vyzantion) as a paradigm of power and opulence seeking patronage and royal marriages from the City of Vyzantion. In the twelfth century their ambitions became much more grandiose, and led to formation of what they called the 'Holy Roman Empire' claiming the inheritance of the glory days of Old Rome. To take an inheritance, however, the ancestor must be dead, and the survival of the Roman Empire in the East was somewhat problematic. At first, the ideological expedient was to claim that with the schism between the Roman and Orthodox churches and supposed decadence, the Roman Empire was morally dead, despite its semblance of sometimes robust life. Wolf's expedient went further, by attempting to deny the empire's existence stripping it of its very name. He could only do that from his place after the final fall, for during its life, its people held to their true Roman heritage with all due tenacity, as some Greek speakers have done into modern times. From as early as the

Assorted middle Byzantine era mace heads found in the Balkans. All are represented to a common scale. The material of the majority of surviving examples are iron, but there are rare bronze ones too. Besides the shapes shown here, there are multi-spiked globular examples corroborating pictures in manuscripts. These were evidently fitted with wooden shafts.

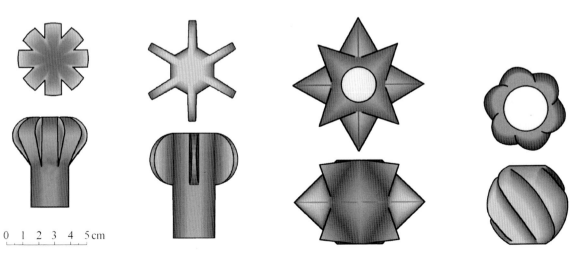

0 1 2 3 4 5cm

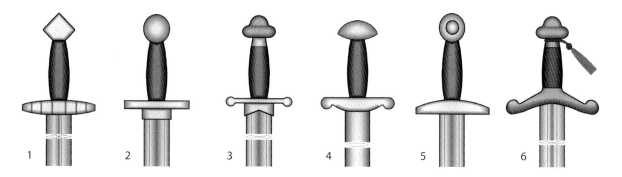

first century AD the empire's residents called it 'Rômania'. The adjectives for that were *Rômaikos* and *Rômios*, and to this day, descendants of the Greek-speaking population which had continued in Ionia, the portion of Anatolia bordering the Aegean Sea, who were expelled by the Turks in the early twentieth century, still call themselves 'Romiosi'. So what is 'Byzantine'? Properly used, it should refer to anything pertaining to the City of Vyzantion, and that is the manner in which it will be used in this volume.

Historical background

The sack of the city of Rome in the fifth century happened largely because Old Rome and the western provinces had increasingly become seen as no longer at the core of the political and economic life of the empire since Constantine I designated an ancient Greek city in Thrace as the new capital in 330 AD, and renamed it the City of Constantine (Kônstantinopolis). The rulers of the Roman Empire were never content to wave the West goodbye. Roman forces fought to recover and hold Italy for the empire with varying degrees of success right through to the late twelfth century. The most determined and successful effort to recover imperial territory was under Justinian I (528–65). From the late sixth century to the end of the ninth century the concerns of the rulers were rather more pressing and closer to home. After Justinian, the ancient rivalry with Persia dominated military matters until it was conclusively settled with the destruction of the Sassanian Empire by Emperor Herakleios in 629. Along the way one of the most important monuments of Roman military literature was created around 602, the *Stratêgikon*, sometimes attributed to the emperor and successful general Maurikios. The *Stratêgikon* was to remain influential right through the middle Byzantine period. The rejoicing was short lived, however, as a new wave of northern barbarians culminated in the Avars besieging the capital itself in 628. The fourth-century walls were more than enough to deter them, although the residents of Konstantinopolis themselves were of the opinion that the Virgin Mary, whose likeness had been paraded about the walls, deserved the credit. At about the same time a much more serious threat arose in the East with the advent of Islam. These newly proselytized Warriors of God conquered the southern and eastern provinces in a remarkably short time. It is commonly accepted that resistance in these areas was undermined by widespread disaffection prompted by religious policies emanating from Constantinople, which had tried to impose centralized Orthodoxy on a region that had very diverse traditions of Christianity, as well as substantial enclaves of older religions. Muslim successes led to them mounting repeated sieges of the city between 668 and 677. Again, the walls of Theodosios were more than equal to the task, but could not have remained so indefinitely against

A far-from-comprehensive sample of sword fittings shown in pictorial sources. 1: tenth century (ivory triptych, Hermitage). 2–5: early eleventh century (*Menologion of Basil II*). 6: later eleventh century (Dafnê Monastery, Chios). Blade forms include pillow section (4) and fullered with grooves ranging from narrow (1), medium (6) to broad (2, 3, 5). (2) and (3) have sleeves which encircle the mouth of the scabbard when sheathed. Other eleventh-century pictures also show what may be either a tassel or lanyard attached to the pommel (6) or at the join between grip and pommel.

continuing assaults. This prospect was forestalled by the schism in Islam and ensuing civil war that created the division between Sunni and Shi'a, and ended the first Muslim expansion into Anatolia.

No sooner had stable borders been established with Islam than the empire was racked internally by an argument over whether the use of religious icons constituted idolatry. The seriousness with which Eastern Orthodoxy of the time took such religious debates, and the fact that the emperor had a crucial role at the centre of the church, meant that for a century the empire was violently divided against itself, body and soul. At the end of the ninth century the issue was resolved in favour of icons, and a period of stability and restoration ensued under the Macedonian emperors.

Emperor Leo VI reformed the legal system. More significantly for our interest, he revived the study of military science at the highest levels. It is evident, despite the disruptions of the preceding century, that the development of new military techniques and adaptation to new circumstances had continued. Leo's contribution was to have these recorded and codified for the first time since the *Stratêgikon*. Leo's *Taktika* preserves those portions of the *Stratêgikon* that were till relevant, and adds the new developments, including the first mention of lamellar armour. Leo was succeeded by his son, Kônstantinos VII 'Born in the Purple' (Porphyrogennêtos). Constantine Porphyrogennêtos continued his father's literary activities, but on the military side his contribution is confined to a manual on imperial participation in military expeditions, which tells us much about the imperial encampment and arrangements, but nothing about ordinary soldiery.

The third quarter of the tenth century was an erratic period for imperial administration, but an important one for this study. Two generals who had proved themselves under Constantine VII undertook to write military manuals. The more significant of these was Nikêforos Fôkas, who had a short period on the imperial throne between 963 and 969. His manual, *A Composition on Warfare*, (more commonly known by a modern Latin title,

The wide plains of central Anatolia were excellent terrain for cavalry operations, as may be seen in this picture. The building in the distance is Sari Han, a lightly fortified caravansarai built by the Seljuk Turks following the example of the way stations maintained to serve the imperial post. (Author's photograph)

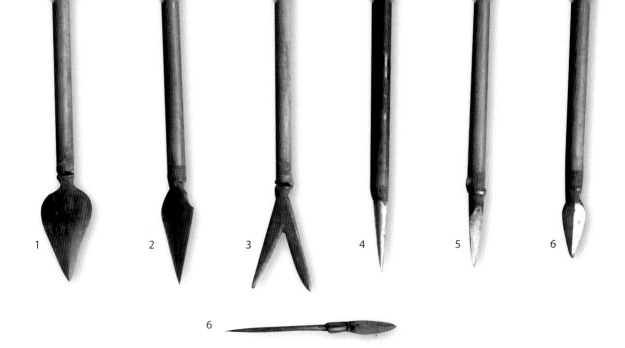

1 2 3 4 5 6

6

Praecepta Militaria) also shows a combination of continuities with and revisions of what has gone before, which tell us much of both his knowledge and his pragmatic experience. The *Taktika* of the second of these later tenth-century generals, Nikêforos Ouranos, owes a great deal to the *Composition on Warfare*, but also shows the benefit of Ouranos' campaign experience.

Throughout late antiquity and the earlier Middle Ages the primary cultural influences on the empire came from the east, especially from Persia, despite the wars, and the destruction of the Sassanian Empire, and despite Iran's incorporation into the new Muslim caliphate. The extent of these influences cannot be underestimated, taking in religion, diverse aspects of everyday life, especially clothing, and also military matters.

In 975 Basil II took the imperial throne. Basil was a man with austere personal habits, who ruled with consistency and firmness. Over the course of 50 years on the Golden Throne he stabilized imperial administration and campaigned effectively to expand the empire's borders to the greatest extent they had achieved since the seventh century. Basil was not an innovator by any means. His contribution was to consolidate, and to implement more consistently policies and practices developed or codified in the earlier tenth century. Basil was unfortunately followed by a series of much less effective rulers who ultimately squandered all of his gains and more. Initially events were merely mixed. Large areas of Sicily were wrested from Muslim control, and the Armenian homeland was brought back under imperial sovereignty. In contrast, territory in Italy, recovered for the Roman Empire by Justinian's campaigns, was gradually whittled away by encroachments of the Normans, who went on to take the newly recovered Sicilian possessions, and then turned their greedy eyes towards Greece. There were similar gradual losses in the East, including Antiokheia (modern Antioch) and Armenian Kilikia. The lowest point was the 'Terrible Day', the disastrous defeat at the battle of Manzikert, which resulted in the loss of the majority of Anatolia to the Seljuk Turks in 1071. Shattering as the defeat at Manzikert was, the empire might still have held its core territories but for almost a decade of civil wars in which rivals contended for the throne.

The civil wars were eventually won in 1081 by another competent general, Alexios Komnênos, and only just in time, as the Normans set their sights on richer pickings in the Balkans. The civil wars had left the empire impoverished and its army in disarray. Nor were the divisions in the aristocracy really eliminated, yet Alexios was able to fend off the Normans and consolidate his power – and, again, only just in time as the armies of the crusade arrived on the borders of the empire. Happily, Alexios proved up to the challenge, moving them on towards Syria, and on the way making good use of them to recover Nikaia for the empire, and extracting a pledge that they would return another recent loss, the city of Antioch, to the control of Constantinople. Until 1118 Alexios continued his work to stabilize the empire both militarily and organizationally.

Alexios' two successors both proved also to be reasonably effective rulers and competent military commanders. Building upon the stability created by his father, Iôannês (John) II set out to recover lost ground, especially to the East. He regained control of Kilikia, and forced the multi-ethnic, Frankish-ruled Principality of Antioch to honour its pledge of allegiance to Kônstantinopolis. Iôannês also seems to have reformed the life of the court, and we can only speculate about how much more he might have achieved had he not died prematurely of septicaemia from an accidental arrow wound.

Manuelos Komnênos set out to carry on the good work of his predecessors, but had somewhat mixed results. His early attempt to continue advances in the East by attacking the Seljuk sultanate based in Ikonion (Konya) failed, and there were renewed problems with Western armies travelling East to join the Crusades. After this, Manuelos turned his attention to the West and the recovery of territory in Italy. This achieved Roman control of Bari and much of Apulia by 1156, but unfortunately political incompetence by the expeditionary force's commander, which alienated allies, meant that these gains were short lived. Activities in the northern Balkans proved to be rather more successful, culminating in a major victory over the Hungarians at Semlin in 1167. Manuelos is said to have introduced western practices to the army, especially to the cavalry.

The political situation of the empire became increasingly difficult as the twelfth century advanced. Assorted western entities were growing in power. These included the 'Holy Roman Empire' and the maritime Italian city-states. The growth of the Italian cities – Pisa, Genoa and especially Constantinople's old colony, Venice – was particularly problematical, for they steadily nibbled away the empire's greatest source of wealth – trade, especially in high value exotic goods such as silk and spices. The emperors tried to use time-honoured military/diplomatic tactics of playing one off against the other. Unfortunately the only way this could be done was by the granting of trade concessions, which only had the result of further reducing Roman revenues from trade and customs duties. Late in his reign Manuelos tried another direction, stripping various Italians of their trading rights and expelling them from the city. This proved in the long term to be even more counterproductive, leading the Italians to redouble their efforts and scheming to strip away Roman trade and possessions in the Balkans. The ultimate expression of this was Venice's hijack of the Fourth Crusade to sack Zara and then Constantinople in 1204.

The empire's tendency to look to the East for its models of cultural sophistication had declined in the late eleventh century. The cultural and intellectual vigour that had characterized the Arab realm in the early centuries of the Islamic era had faded, and al-Islamiyya had much less novelty to offer.

The rise of the West and the great movements of crusade and trade meant that some of the need for novelty began to be satisfied from that direction as the twelfth century progressed, although the majority of cultural transmission was still from Rômania to the West.

The last 20 years leading up to the Fourth Crusade was a tragic period. The dynasty of the Komnênoi petered out with two emperors who only lasted three years each, and achieved nothing beneficial. The rulers of the Angelos family who followed fared little better, as the political elite of the empire was riven with dissension about how to deal with the western powers and threats. In the Roman Empire such dissension was never merely a matter of debate, but of coups, counter-coups and spontaneous civil and military unrest. Thus the elite of the empire proved incapable of forestalling the machinations of the Venetians, nor of resisting effectively once the armies of the Fourth Crusade had been diverted against the Queen of Cities.

The military background

The fully professional armies of early Rome were long gone by the beginning of the middle Byzantine era. There were still professional units based in the capital and major cities, but now the majority of any major expeditionary army was composed of part-time troops whose families held agricultural land in exchange for military service, further augmented by temporary levies and mercenaries.

The Roman army in the earlier period had been the infantry. Cavalry had been the province of foreign auxiliaries to begin with, and even when better established had only very specific and limited roles. Towards the end of Late Antiquity the empire faced new threats, and the army confronted unfamiliar military methods. Primary amongst these was the increased use of cavalry amongst Rome's enemies, and not just any cavalry, but heavily armoured horsemen riding armoured horses equipped with stirrups. The army lost no time in fully matching these eastern cavalry techniques. The Roman adoption of the stirrup in the later sixth century dramatically changed the balance of

A large garrison fortress guarding the north end of the Bosphoros, probably built in the Komnenian era. Its large size in part shows the greater economic strength of the empire in this period, but the expanse of its interior also suggests it may have been a major base for cavalry operations. (Author's photograph)

effectiveness in the forces, making the cavalry the pre-eminent offensive arm in the open battlefield. Even before this, the Romans had been fielding more heavily armoured horsemen riding armoured horses, as is shown by the lamellar horse's chest-piece from Dura Europos. In the wake of this, the infantry in the field became more of a moving fortress that often served to provide a solid base for the swifter striking of the mounted arm. It also made an essential focus for enemy action, for, of course, Roman cavalry was no less amorphous and capable of evading countermeasures than that of any other nation. In principle, the infantry retained the same capacity for offensive action it had always had, but the situations in which that offensive capability could be applied were fewer than they had been. Along with such cavalry methods, the Romans also enthusiastically adopted eastern archery techniques, to such a degree that the author of the *Stratêgikon* could speak of the thumb draw, devised originally by the nomadic horse-tribes for mounted use, as being the 'Roman draw', in contrast to the three-fingered draw of the Persians. From this time, as much was expected of Roman horse archers as of those of the nomads.

The recovery from the so-called 'Dark Age', which began in the eighth century, led the Roman army to re-acquaint itself with two ancient, oriental forms of armour – scale and lamellar. Both are made of plates of solid material, which may be metal, horn or leather and which may be of very similar size, shape and form. The consistent difference between them in our period is that scales were fastened to a single substrate, a garment of cloth or leather and overlapped downward, while lamellae were first fastened together in rows and then tied together, normally overlapping upwards. Like mail, these armour pieces with their numerous, but modestly sized identical components had the advantage of being amenable to small-scale production units. Unlike mail, they both offered much higher levels of protection. The manuals of the beginning of the tenth century do not make much distinction between infantry and cavalry armour, but the status of the cavalry as the elite arm meant that they had first claim on these superior forms of defence, and this is explicitly acknowledged in the later tenth-century manuals. The combination of lightness, flexibility and relative cheapness of lamellar made of hide allowed the Roman army to embrace the practice of armouring the horses. This made for another leap in the cavalry's effectiveness, as they

 THE PRESS OF BATTLE

The success of any army on campaign hinges upon the effective coordination of its various component parts. In the case of the Roman army of the middle Byzantine era this meant not only coordinating cavalry with infantry, but ensuring that the specialized components of each of these arms worked well together. The speed of the cavalry arm and the fluidity of its engagements made this all the more critical. The medium weight unit called *koursôres* had a particularly diverse and important role in this respect. *Koursôres* had to be well enough equipped to be capable of engaging in direct hand-to-hand combat with opposing cavalry and smaller, less ordered groups of infantry, and yet had to be light and agile to operate flexibly over considerable distances and diverse terrain. Hence, mail was the most common armour for such troops, with scale as an alternative. When functioning as *defensores*, as shown in this plate at right, it was their job to cover the retreat of other units as they returned to base. Here they ride out to repel enemy horsemen pursuing lightly armoured archers, who are returning to cover behind an infantry block in order to restock their ammunition. The openings in an infantry formation, like the gates in a fortified camp, were choke points where things could go seriously awry, with units coming and going simultaneously. Pragmatically, it seems likely that troops would keep to the right when passing in such situations.

were able to commit themselves to attacking more solid enemy formations and more sustained close-quarters combat with greater confidence than before. The eleventh and twelfth centuries were a period of economic growth, and evidence suggests that this meant that across the period the army had a tendency to be somewhat better equipped than hitherto. Of course war is a voracious beast, and there are notable exceptions to this tendency, as in 1081 when Alexios Komnênos was obliged to requisition civilian clothing to make fake surcoats in order to conceal his troops' lack of real armour. The Fourth Crusade, the consequential Latin occupation of Kônstantinopolis lasting almost 60 years and the permanent impoverishment of the empire radically interrupted the culture of the army as much as any area of life. As one illustration, lamellar was never again seen amongst the equipment of the Roman Army.

Force structure and ranks

The *tagma* or *stratos* was any expeditionary force. Its size was determined by the nature of the campaign traded off against the economic and logistical constraints on the manpower that could be raised. It was commanded by a *stratêgos* or general. The subdivisions of the cavalry seem all to have been done by threes. Thus a *tagma* was divided into three *tourmai* or *merê*, each commanded, unsurprisingly, by a *tourmarkhês* or *merarkhos*. Each *tourma* was split into three *droungoi* or *moirai*, led by a *droungarios* or *moirarkhos*. Below him were three *komêtes* (counts), each commanding a 'banner' (*vandon*) which in the cavalry was also called *allagion*. The size of equestrian units could vary much more than that of the foot soldiers. The basic *allagion* was 50-strong, and this was apparently considered normal, but some, notably the imperial and Thracian *allagia*, could number up to 400. At the basic level, then, the units were built on *allagia* of 50, a *droungos* of 150, a *tourma* of 450 and the *tagma* of 1,350. As the larger *allagia* were, it seems, uncommon, the upper limit was probably much less than the 10,800 that such multiplications would suggest. Nikêforos Fôkas stated that 5,000 cavalry and the aid of God were all a general needed. The equestrian battle line was conventionally much like the infantry block, being 100 men wide and five lines deep, and subdivided with the same sequence of junior officers – *kentarkhoi* (the old centurion), *pentakontarkhoi* (commander of 50), *dekarkhoi* (leader of 10) and *pentarkhoi* (head of five). These officers seem to have been apointed ad hoc, although presumably the *kentarkhos* and *pentarkhos* of each line of battle were the *komêtes* of the two *allagia* that made up that line. Maintaining time-honoured practice, the primary functional unit of the cavalry expeditionary army was the unit of two troopers plus groom/servant who shared a tent.

The standard form of the middle-Byzantine military banner. The body represented the *meros* or *tourma* and carried some simple, often geometric emblem. The tails were then colour-coded for each subunit. The two outer tails probably represented the *droungos*, and then the tails between (sometimes as many as five in especially large armies) bore a unique combination of colours for each 'banner' (*vandon*).

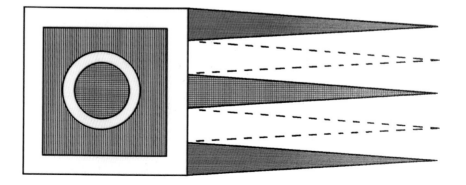

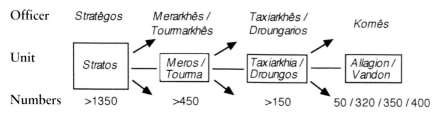

Permanent organizational divisions

Officer	Stratêgos	Merarkhês / Tourmarkhês	Taxiarkhês / Droungarios	Komês
Unit	Stratos	Meros / Tourma	Taxiarkhia / Droungos	Allagion / Vandon
Numbers	>1350	>450	>150	50 / 320 / 350 / 400

Temporary battlefield divisions

Officer	Kentarkhos / Hekatontarkhos	Pentakosiarkhos	Dekarkhos	Pentarkhos
Unit	Kentarkhia	Penta-kosiarkhia	Dekarkhia	Pentarkhia
Numbers	100	50	10	5

A summary of the force structure of a cavalry army of this period. The upper structure is the permanent organizational structure, while the lower is the system for a battlefield array.

The general staff had a full range of functionary ranks. *Mandatôres* carried the orders down the chain of command. *Minsôres* or *minsouratôres* were surveyors who went ahead of the marching army to lay out the camp. There were also banner bearers (*vandoforoi*) and trumpeters (*voukinatores*). Training was supervised by drill-masters called *kampidoktores*, who carried a distinctive baton called the *kampidiktorion*.

CHRONOLOGY

Mid-sixth century	The adoption of the stirrup commences the process whereby the cavalry becomes established as the premier offensive segment of the Roman army. The *Stratêgikon* of Maurikios/Urbikios (*c.* 602) embodies the completion of this process.
628	Avars besiege Constantinople.
633–50	Loss of Roman possessions in Syria and Egypt.
668–77	Repeated Muslim sieges of Constantinople.
886–912	Leôn VI ('Leo the Wise'/*Sophos*).
c. **895**	Composition of the *Taktika* of Leôn.
913–59	Kônstantinos VII ('Born in the purple'/*Porphyrogennêtos*). Kônstantinos VII presided over a veritable imperial publishing industry, including a detailed treatise on imperial military expeditions and an inventory of the *matériel* of the Cyprus expedition.
939	A large expedition is launched with the aim of taking Cyprus back from the Muslims. It is unsuccessful.
c. **950**	Likely date for the composition of the *Syllogê Taktikôn*.

959–63	Reign of Rômanos II.
963–69	Reign of Nikêforos II Fôkas. The *Composition on Warfare* (*Praecepta Militaria*) appears to have been written while Nikêforos was emperor.
969–76	Reign of Iôannês I Tzimiskês.
976–1025	Reign of Basil II (later called 'the Bulgar-slayer'/*Bulgaroktonos*), sole emperor.
999–1007	Nikêforos Ouranos serves as governor of the province of Antiokheia (Antioch) in Syria. His *Taktika* was composed during this period.
1014	Basil crushes the forces of the Bulgarian kingdom at the battle of Kleidôn. Bulgaria never again poses any serious threat to the empire.
1020s	First Norman incursions into Roman territory in southern Italy.
1025–28	Reign of Kônstantinos VIII ('Born in the purple'/*Porphyrogennêtos*).
1028–34	Reign of Rômanos III Argyros.
1034–41	Mikhailos IV ('the Paphlagonian'/*Paphlagonos*).
1038–43	Eastern Sicily recovered from Muslim control. Shortly afterwards it is lost again to Norman encroachment.
1042	Zôê ('Born in the purple'/*Porphyrogennêta*).
1042–54	Reign of Kônstantinos IX ('the Duellist'/*Monomakhos*). How this emperor got his nickname is a mystery, for he had no particular martial talent.
1045	Armenian heartland re-incorporated into the empire.
1052	Edessa and surrounding region re-incorporated into the empire.
1055–56	Reign of Theodôra ('Born in the purple'/*Porphyrogennêta*).
1056–57	Reign of Mikhailos VI Bringas.
1057–59	Reign of Isaakios I Komnênos.
1059–67	Reign of Kônstantinos X Doukas.
1070s	Norman expansion begins to encroach on Roman territory in the Balkans.

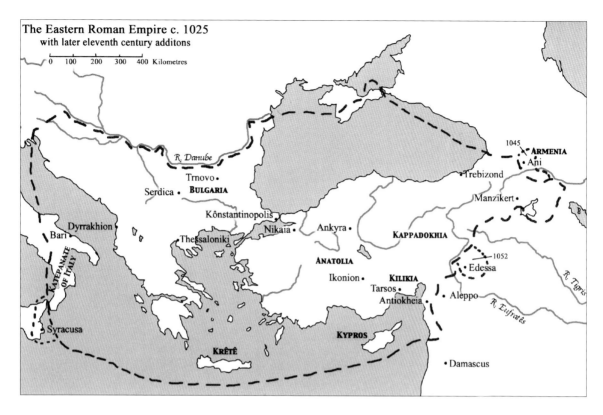

The Eastern Roman Empire c. 1025
with later eleventh century additons

0 100 200 300 400 Kilometres

R. Danube
Trnovo •
Serdica • **BULGARIA**
Kônstantinopolis •
Dyrrakhion • Nikaia •
Bari • Thessaloniki •
KATEPANATE OF ITALY
Syracusa •
KRÊTÊ
Ankyra •
KAPPADOKHIA
ANATOLIA
Ikonion • **KILIKIA**
Tarsos •
Antiokheia •
KYPROS
1045 **ARMENIA**
• Ani
• Trebizond
Manzikert •
1052
• Edessa
Aleppo • R. Tigris
R. Eufrates
• Damascus

1067–71	Reign of Rômanos IV Diogenês.
1071	Roman army severely defeated by the Seljuk Turks at Manzikert due to divisions in command. Rômanos IV Diogenês captured and killed shortly after. This defeat resulted in the permanent loss of most of the empire's Anatolian territory. Normans capture Bari, the last Roman outpost in Italy.
1071–78	Reign of Mikhailos VII Doukas. Mikhailos VII attempted to curb Norman incursions by diplomatic methods, particularly by a marriage alliance.
1078–81	Reign of Nikêforos III Botaneiatês. During Botaneiatês' reign the Normans resume their encroachments onto the Greek islands.
1081–1118	Reign of Alexios I Komnênos. Alexios triumphed after a period of civil war that severely damaged the army, and led to a dramatic increase in the use of foreign mercenaries in preference to regular Roman troops.
1081	An army led by Alexios I is defeated by Normans at Dyrrakhion.
1098	The armies of the First Crusade arrive at Constantinople. Alexios hastens them across the Bosforos into Anatolia and sends them to recapture Nikaia from the Turks. Roman forces pre-empt the storming of the city by the crusaders by taking the

The Roman Empire around the middle of the eleventh century – at its greatest extent during the Middle Ages.

Nikaian surrender directly. This causes considerable resentment amongst the westerners, and is used as a pretext for repudiating agreements they had made, notably to return Antiokheia to the control of Kônstantinopolis.

1118–43	Reign of Iôannês II Komnênos. Iôannês sets out to continue the work of stabilization and reconquest begun by his father. He is noted for his equestrian skill.
1138	Iôannês II leads a large army to the East, re-asserting Vyzantion's suzerainty over Armenian Kilikia and the crusader principality of Antioch. During this expedition nobles of the Constantinopolitan court compete against those of Antioch in the first recorded tournament in the East.
1143	John dies of septicaemia resulting from a wound from his own arrows whilst out hunting during a campaign.
1143–80	Reign of Manuelos I Komnênos. Manuelos continues his father's generally effective campaigning in both the East and West, and is credited with westernizing the military methods used by the army, particularly encouraging western equipment for the cavalry. Manuelos enters into an alliance with the German 'Holy Roman Empire' against the Hohenstaufen kingdom of Sicily and Italy.
1147	Launching of the Second Crusade.
1148	Normans begin to permanently occupy territory on the Greek mainland.
1153–56	Imperial troops attempt to regain control of southern Italy. Initially successful, the campaign ends with defeat at Brindisi.
1156	Kilikian Armenians under T'oros rebel against imperial rule.
1158	Manuelos brings rebellious Kilikia back under the control of Kônstantinopolis.
1159	In the wake of the end of the rebellion in Kilikia, Reynald de Chatillon, Prince of Antiokheia, makes submission to the emperor, who enters the city in triumph.
1176	Turks inflict a severe defeat on the Roman army at Myriokefalon. This ends attempts to recover the Anatolian losses of the battle of Manzikert.
1180–83	Reign of Alexios II Komnênos.
1182	Some Western residents of Kônstantinopolis are massacred in a riot that may have imperial backing.

1182–85	Reign of Andronikos I Komnênos. He tries to reform the bureaucracy and reduce the influence of the great families and of westerners. His repressive measures alienate the aristocracy and then the populace, leading to his overthrow.
1184	Andronikos makes an alliance with Sala'ad-din, which would have partitioned the Levant between the empire and the Ayyubid sultanate.
1185–95	First reign of Isaakios II Angelos. Isaakios and his son Alexios III have no ability for, nor inclination towards, administration, and preside over a regime of excess and dissolution which further weakens the empire.
1195–1203	Reign of Alexios III Angelos. Friction and violence between the natives and western residents within the empire increase.
1203–04	Second reign of Isaakios II (his co-emperor is Alexios IV). Isaakios II is reinstated by western intervention, but the demands of the foreigners offend the populace, who reject these rulers and elevate the anti-western Alexios Mourtzouphlos.
1204	Reign of Alexios V Mourtzouphlos. The empire is now too weak to make any serious resistance to western forces and falls to the hijacked Fourth Crusade in August.

RECRUITMENT

The Roman army of the middle Byzantine era necessarily drew upon a wide diversity in sources of manpower. For the cavalry arm, while this observation was true ethnically, the class composition was inevitably more restricted. Certain considerations mentioned in the manuals are timeless. Only the best physical specimens were to be preferred, and none older than 40 years of age. Recruits ought also, as far as could be determined, to be of good character and honest.

At the beginning of the tenth century the thematic forces that made up the bulk of the army were drawn from a pool of families who held *strateia*, that is, who owed military service in connection with tenure of land. While some infantry was probably derived from this source, it was overwhelmingly true for the cavalry. Fundamentally, this was because a cavalryman was expected to bring equestrian skills and experience to his term of service, and to maintain those skills between campaigns by his own means. He therefore had to maintain a mount, something which always required a significant agricultural surplus, as well as using time spared from labour on the land. *Strateia* service was hereditary, passing from one individual to another within a family. Such men were recorded on the *adnoumia*, or muster rolls, maintained by the provincial commander. In addition to age or infirmity, serious crimes were cause for the registered man to be struck off the roll. In such a case, his obligation would be transferred, in the first instance to another suitable member of his (extended) family, or if no such person was available, it would be commuted to a monetary payment, or temporarily or permanently assigned elsewhere. Similarly, the *strateia* would be reassigned where such a family died out. Where possible, an empty *strateia* would be transferred to a stratiotic household who had gained members who could discharge the service. Otherwise, it would be assigned to another capable local family, either voluntarily or by imposition. Another option exercised from the capital was to resettle areas where there was a quantity of stratiotic lands in need of tenancy. Such settlers could be drawn from other areas within the empire, a policy that was sometimes used to alleviate overpopulation, and at others to forestall potential dissension. Resettlement was repeatedly imposed upon segments of the Armenian population for this reason. Other settlers were immigrants to the empire, such as the Arab tribe called Banu Habib who were taken in by Constantine VII, and Saxon families who fled to the empire after the Norman conquest of England. Remarkably, one last category of settler given stratiotic lands comprised prisoners of war; presumably their obligations were to be discharged in some manner that would not compromise operational security. Various authorities stipulated the value of land sufficient for a *strateia*. Nikêforos II decreed a minimum of an estate worth 16 pounds of gold, or 1,152 nomismata, in order to maintain one of his heavy *katafraktoi*. The current estimate is that such a property would have been worked by something in the vicinity of 30 families. The lighter types of horsemen were expected to have lands worth no less than about half that, and so tenants of 15 or so families. In addition to providing mounts, money and supplies, such estates must also have offered a pool of experienced manpower which might be drawn upon for support roles such as grooms, horse-doctors or baggage-beast handlers. In addition to cases of incapacity, as noted above, there was an increasing tendency through the later tenth and eleventh centuries for *strateia* obligations to be commuted into a cash equivalent; this was added to military tax revenues to fund more reliable tagmatic units or to hire mercenaries.

The sources of recruits for the standing tagmatic units were equally various. Just as in many another societies right up to today, military service must have been an attractive option for males who found themselves short of prospects. Even then, such men must have come from a more affluent social background, one that had afforded early equestrian experience, although perhaps exceptional determination and talent would have served the advancement of some from less privileged sectors of society. In the countryside, tagmatic recruitment was not so much a matter of the 'younger son syndrome' seen in the West, since inheritance of land within the empire was partitive rather than singly by primogeniture, so it must have been more a matter of choice on one hand, or dire necessity in some cases where partitive inheritance would render a farm too small to be viable. Tagmatic forces were also composed to some degree of foreign troops. It is not entirely appropriate to characterize these as 'mercenaries', since at this time such foreigners were incorporated into the Roman army's established structure and methods, rather than forming their own units, and undertook longer-term service. A better modern comparison might be the Gurkhas in the British Army, since the foreigners serving in the imperial army likewise often came from places with a long-standing and quasi-colonial relationship with Constantinople. Examples of this include, again, the Armenians, and also Georgians, Bulgarians and southern Rus'.

Just which of the three arms of the cavalry (archers, *koursôres* or *katafraktoi*) a rider joined would depend, all other things being equal, upon what gear the man brought with him to the muster. The other prime factor was, of course, his skills and aptitudes. It must be presumed that intelligent officers would rate this more highly than gear when assigning troops, using official supply to remedy equipment deficiencies for men who showed particular courage and ability for the hand-to-hand combat roles. Men would also be assigned, and transferred while on campaign, in order to achieve an optimum balance of forces.

Soldiery was not all the army needed, of course. There was also the support staff – muleteers, wagoneers, doctors for man and horse, and each pair of 'spear companions' had a man to serve as servant and groom. With many of these men requiring less specific skill or experience, the net could be cast much wider. For thematic expeditions, such ancillary manpower would have been levied from amongst the local population. Often, particularly for the cavalry, these functions must have been filled by youths or boys from stratiotic households who were too young to take up full military duties, or those who could be spared from tenant families, as has been noted.

CONDITIONS OF SERVICE

The Roman forces of this era, both cavalry and infantry, were divided into two broad categories – part time and full time. The part-time troops consisted of men who belonged to families that held military lands, or *strateia*, and therefore were obliged to keep in regular training, acquire and maintain some or all of their own equipment, and muster at the first call-up. Full-time troops were those standing units maintained primarily in the capital, and smaller units based in large provincial administrative centres.

Men discharging *strateia* obligations, or *strateioumenoi*, were expected to maintain their skills by training between campaigns. The local *stratêgos* had the responsibility of supervising the ongoing training of troops on the muster lists, so presumably from time to time he would assemble the enrolled troops to revise their drills and assess their skills. *Strateioumenoi* were also required to serve for longer periods and farther afield than the infantry levies once a campaign was launched. At earlier stages, or when the expeditionary force was campaigning nearby, the estate bearing the *strateia* was expected to furnish some supplies for the man discharging the service and his mount. Thereafter, and farther afield, the troops were sustained by forage and requisitioned supplies. Roman armies of this era did not normally campaign over winter, so the *strateioumenoi* enjoyed a standard demobilization of at least three months for the low season.

Troops recruited from a given locality were grouped together in common units. This was in part to ensure that they had things in common to bind them together through the privations of service, and partly to reduce the potential for infiltration by spies and saboteurs. The cavalry equivalent of the infantry *kontouvernion* was a pair of cavalrymen who shared a tent and assistance of a servant/groom, an arrangement called 'spear companions'. When they came from the same village the troopers may well have already made an alliance prior to call-up and brought a familiar servant with them.

While officers sometimes had the benefit of campbeds, the common soldier presumably laid his bedding out on the ground in the manner of these pilgrims in the courtyard of a shrine. The motif of three unequal stripes is typical of such domestic textiles. Ordinary soldiers' bedding must have been very similar. (Monastery of Dionysiou, Mount Athos)

Full-time troops formed the defensive garrisons of major towns, and a larger force was stationed in the capital. As well as being on hand in preparation for sudden attacks, an important role for these garrison forces must have been to form a nucleus of well-trained and drilled troops to pass on a standard of performance to the *strateioumenoi* and levies once they were mobilized. As professional soldiery with no other means of support, they were maintained by the state, although if they served elsewhere they might well have brought equipment of their own, and in any case would be sure to upgrade their gear whenever they were able, even if they had been initially equipped at state expense.

Unlike the early imperial era when a set period of service was expected, in this period the term of service seems to have been very pragmatic for both full-time soldiers and *strateioumenoi*. Men served as long as they were fit for duty, and sometimes even longer by accident, for the manuals mention the need to review the muster rolls from time to time in order to weed out men who were no longer in a position to serve, as well as to add new recruits.

All troops received some payment for their service in addition to their maintenance. There seems to have been a common tendency for pay for long-term enrolled troops to be very irregular, as witnessed by outbreaks of unrest when pay was not forthcoming, and Constantine VII's attempt to set it on a four-year cycle. On special occasions, however, pay could be much more regular and frequent. The expedition to Crete in 949 paid one (gold) nomisma per month for four months to each ordinary soldier, apparently without distinction between cavalry and infantry, while the cavalry from Thrace and Macedonia got two nomismata.

Discipline was, of course, an essential element of military service, and all the manuals have substantial sections dealing with military laws and penalties. All the offences we would expect are noted: ignoring officers and orders, disobeying orders, and desertion and betrayal to the enemy of plans or cities and fortresses. To these are added the theft, loss or unauthorized disposal of equipment and livestock, neglect of equipment, the theft of public money such as taxes and military levies, and claiming allowances dishonestly.

B **MEDICAL SERVICES**

With a great reservoir of ancient experience to draw on, the Roman army from the tenth century onwards had medical services that were as well organized as the other aspects of its activities. The knowledge that rescue and care were available is a major factor in encouraging troops to more confident endeavours, and steadying them if the tide of battle begins to turn adversely. Yet the mobility of the cavalry arm made the provision of such services both easier and more difficult than for the infantry. Where the battle was conducted with primarily cavalry forces, or with a linear infantry front rather than in a square, the field hospital was to be located two kilometres or more behind the front. The less severely wounded horsemen who were still mounted could make their own way to treatment stations, thus easing the burden on the medical corps, but when a cavalryman was unhorsed he was likely to be farther from the field hospital. Hence, the *daipotatoi*, or ambulance men, were supplied with their own mounts for the recovery of fallen horsemen.

The manuals mention that the saddles of these horses were to be fitted with an additional stirrup on the near (left) side to allow the *daipotatos* to mount once he had the wounded man seated. They were also to carry a flask of water to help revive casualties. The field hospitals had, of course, a full staff of doctors and orderlies to tend the men, and presumably also some horse doctors to treat wounded mounts. Doubtless, the difficulty of replacing losses with appropriately trained horses while on campaign meant that they were the beneficiaries of care close to that which the troopers received.

The universal and time-honoured penalty of death was imposed for desertion and treachery. Mutilation, such as the cutting off of nose or ears, were used for serious offenses, while scourging was the basic penalty for many lesser transgressions. This punishment was normally administered by the immediate superior officer of the offender. In certain cases a trooper's immediate superior would also be punished for his fault, such as if a man neglected his arms and armour whilst on leave. The actual quantity of lashes for any offence seems to have been left to custom, or the preferences of the officers concerned. Leo advises against excessive harshness as being likely to contribute to loss of morale and unrest in the ranks. Fines were also imposed for transgressions whose effects were financial. Thus, for example, a man who dishonestly claimed an allowance, such as for mobile service while the army was in winter quarters, was required to pay back twice the amount he had falsely gained.

On the positive side, a man who was honest and competent could look forward to earning promotion, sometimes to quite eminent rank, wherever he may have started. It should be noted, though, that good family connections did ease a man's path into the upper officer class, although this must have been a much more prevalent paradigm in the cavalry, simply by virtue of its being the more glamorous and expensive arm.

After service

The sources are largely silent about what became of surviving soldiers after they left service, but some conclusions can be drawn from peripheral evidence. As noted above, the holders of *strateia* were liable to be called up from their farms for as long as they were physically capable of discharging their duty. Thereafter, they simply stayed at home while a younger or fitter member of the family took on the duty or it was commuted to cash. The circumstances of demobilized tagmatic soldiers was much more diverse. The lack of any set period of service meant that a man might leave the army whilst still in his prime. Men were also, of course, invalided out of the service. Those who left in good health or not wholly disabled must have gone into any of the range of civilian labour roles that they were capable of performing. In the early empire 45 years was the age at which a man became a *senex*, an old man, and marked the point at which he was discharged from the army if he had not yet completed the standard term. Since 40 was the maximum enlistment age recorded in the period of this study, it seems likely that 45 was still the retirement point. Another continuity is that retired tagmatic troops still enjoying good health and having no other ties were settled on vacant military lands, in the hope that they might establish families that would broaden the army's pool of manpower. Men who were discharged as invalids for whatever reason necessarily turned to public or private charity. Religious institutions were the primary agencies for such support, and monasteries must have been the refuge for many disabled or infirm elderly soldiers.

BELIEF AND BELONGING

The sense of identity that was embraced by the citizens of the Eastern Roman Empire can be hard for a modern Western person to understand. It was intimately bound up with religion, yet with an intensity that even medieval Westerners found hard to comprehend. For one thing, the common man of

Rômania felt fully entitled to hold and express opinions on issues of doctrine and theology, in contrast to the Western Christian church's paradigm, where such matters were thrashed out by silk-clad old men behind closed doors and then revealed to a grateful but acquiescent laity. The theologians of the Orthodox church did not particularly approve of popular involvement in theological disputation. The outcome of some church councils was as much determined by cudgels in back alleys as by elevated debate and negotiation in marble halls, and the fourth-century theologian, Gregory of Nyssa, remarked with disgust that a trip to the market or bathhouse could lead to a lecture on some obscure theological topic from such lowly fellows as the bread seller or bathhouse attendant.

The compact made with the god of Christianity by Emperor Constantine at the battle of Milvian Bridge ('In this sign you will conquer') resonated throughout society, and right through the army. Yet the idea that with Constantine's bargain the Roman Empire became the vessel through which Christianity would be most perfectly expressed ultimately acted more to the army's cost than to its advantage. On one hand, there was the idea that if it were the 'chosen realm' then God would defend it, provided its citizens were suitably pious, perhaps even without the need for terrestrial armies. This was good for the cults of military saints and the Holy Virgin, but not necessarily good for army recruitment. The concept of 'proper piety' was also not entirely helpful. The habit of soldiers of assuaging the stress of wartime service with drinking, gambling and fornication runs across cultural boundaries, and presented a constant problem within Orthodox religious parameters. Furthermore, Orthodox Christianity has never had anything like the concept of 'holy war' that was contrived by the Church of Rome to justify crusading and the military–religious orders. One result of this was that homicide remained a sin, even when the victims were non-Christian enemies of church and state. Hence, soldiers in the later Roman army spent much of their campaigning time on penance, however token, for having committed murder. Such penance obviously could not be so exacting as to impair the men's functioning, so it must have been similar to the milder monastic practices of *xerofagia* and *hydroposia*, that is, meals without meat and days without wine. Thus, being a soldier in the Eastern Roman Empire must sometimes have entailed being in a somewhat ideologically conflicting twilight zone, neither fully accepted by society, nor wholly supported by the church. This feeling would be assuaged by the fact that the daily life of the army was punctuated by religious rites designed to ensure that the troops were aware of their important role in God's appointed empire, and would not die in a state of sin.

One of the most important foci for personal spirituality in eastern Christianity has always been warrior-saints, most notably Dêmêtrios, George and the two Theodores. Their cults must have had particular resonance for serving soldiers, despite the fact that most of them were martyred for refusing to fight (on behalf of pagan emperors). Warrior-saints are the subject of the most commonly surviving type of less expensive icon, those carved of soapstone, where they are depicted with a degree of contemporary realism that is quite unlike other forms of religious art. This suggests that their devotees felt a degree of affinity with them that was shared with the more remote figures of Jesus or Mary. Warrior-saints are also often found depicted on small, cast bronze crucifixes that survive in some quantity. Such cheap talismanic jewellery must have been a common accessory across the army.

The picture is further complicated by the divergent lifestyles of the tagmatic and thematic armies. The part-time soldiering of the provincial forces must have left them with a direct sense of community – they could see that it was the homes of their families and neighbours they were defending. The nature of the *tagmata* would necessarily have broken this element down, as recruits left their communities across Rômania for the detached microcosm of barracks life in and around Constantinople and major cities. The sense of detachment from the urban civilian community can only have been enhanced by the fact that it fell to units of the army to suppress outbreaks of civil unrest in the capital and major cities. Such rioting was nowhere near as severe nor as brutally repressed in the middle Byzantine period than it had been earlier in the empire, yet still they were sometimes required to slaughter fellow citizens and fellow Christians, who might even have been their neighbours or relatives.

So where did the Roman soldier of the tenth to twelfth centuries find a sense of belonging? Sometimes it undoubtedly lay in shared loyalty to the emperor, at least when he had distinguished himself as a successful military commander – but many were ephemeral and did not do so. Ultimately, for the tagmatic armies especially, the sense of belonging must have fallen upon the institution of the army itself.

TRAINING

As noted elsewhere, the great bulk of the manpower for the empire's cavalry came from families discharging *strateia*, and commonly supplying both man and mount, with some quantity of gear and supplies. One consequence of this was that men usually arrived, even on their first mobilization, already having the essential equestrian skills, and probably some basic martial training as well. Despite all the changes in technology, the equestrian training precepts of the Hellenistic author Xenophon had remained unchallenged, and, indeed, largely continue to apply today. Xenophon declared that 'nothing serves to make so good a seat as the grip of a bare thigh on a sweaty flank.' The ancient Greek and Persian riding style involved sitting well forward with the legs turned out

TRAINING

Cavalry recruits were almost always drawn either from families owing cavalry *strateia*, that is to say, an obligation of military service, or from the more affluent sector of society. Hence, they normally arrived with a basic competency in riding and some equestrian skills transferable to military use from activities like hunting and sports such as the javelin game and *tzikanion*, a very popular ball game very much like modern polocrosse. Yet, those skills would need to be polished and extended to refine them for optimum military utility. Coordinated riding in large groups would be a new skill requiring careful drilling. In archery, for example, the Parthian shot (shooting backwards while riding at speed) was an essential military skill, but of much less use in civilian equestrian activities, and so would need extra practice. Similarly, a recruit, however skilled, would need to acclimatize himself to executing all manoeuvres and actions with the extra encumbrance of armour and spare weaponry. Here on the left, a *kampidoktor*, or drill master, conducts an assessment of the archery skill of a recruit, by having him execute the standard exercise of shooting at a shaft, with a *notarios* (secretary) standing in attendance to record any comments. The archer is clad in basic light battlefield kit, while the *kampidoktor* himself wears a dress *epilôrikion* (surcoat) and carries his *kampidiktorion* or staff of office. The precise form of this baton is unknown. The garb of the *notarios* is not much different from civilian dress of the time. An assessment like this would be required to determine where a man's skills and experience would best be used – amongst the archers, the *koursôres* or skirmishers, or in the close press of the *katafraktoi*.

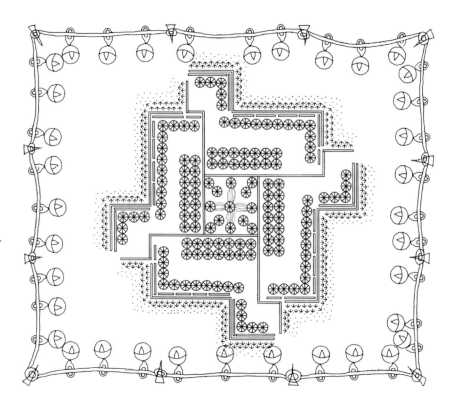

A schematic diagram of the layout of a marching camp according to an eleventh-century manuscript, showing that the old Roman practices continued in use. The grey outer lines represent the ditch. The black inner lines represent the bank. The triangles are caltrops sown between them. The early warning system mentioned in the manuals of bells strung on trip-lines is visible around the outside. The circles are tents. The central cluster is the residence of the commander and his staff. The cavalry were encamped in the middle cluster with the infantry outermost, to make it less likely that a surprise attack would stampede the horses, and to give them time to saddle and arm for a counterattack.

and the feet pointed down to tuck the heels in behind the forelegs. The author can attest to the effectiveness of this riding style, and it continued in use through later periods despite the advent of more substantial legwear, and the adoption of the stirrup within the empire in the late sixth century. (It even survives in the Caucasus today.) In this riding style the stirrups serve primarily as a mounting step (hence the early medieval Greek word for them: *skala* – stair, or ladder) and then, hanging quite loose on the foot, as an emergency aid. As the stirrup became fully integrated into Roman practice, and mounted archery increased in importance, the Central Asian riding style with its shorter stirrups carrying more weight became increasingly common. It allowed shooting over a wider arc, and particularly facilitated the 'Parthian shot' in which the archer loosed an arrow directly behind him. Greater contacts with the West from the later tenth century introduced the less-demanding European chivalric riding style with its low seat and legs thrust well forward in long stirrups. By the mid-twelfth century this method was probably dominant for the most heavily armoured horsemen who no longer employed archery, while the necessity for the widest arc of discharge for bow and javelin would have necessitated the lighter cavalry keeping to the higher and more flexible forms of seat.

With the essential equestrian and weapon skills inculcated from an early age, they were maintained during peacetime by a mixture of hunting, and sports such as the skirmish game with blunt javelins or darts known to the early Romans as *hippika gymnasia* and carried on by the Turks right up to modern times as *jirid*. Another very popular sport for honing equestrian skills in a quasi-combat situation was *tzikanion*. Imported from Persia during the early imperial period, *tzikanion* bore a great resemblance to modern 'polocrosse' – a leather ball was captured, carried and cast by riders each using a small net on a long stick. *Tzikanion* could be extremely violent – the death of Emperor Alexandros in 913 was attributed to exhaustion after a particularly vigorous game, while in the thirteenth century Emperor Iôannes Axoukhos fell from his horse and was trampled to death in a match. In the wake of the Crusades, *tzikanion* had a period of popularity in the south of France as '*chicane*', giving rise to the modern expression 'playing chicken'. There must also have been some method for training and practising for the use of the *kontarion*, or lance, and sword, but these were probably done simply by attacking posts set in the ground, as per infantry drills.

Having men arrive at their muster point with these basic skills in hand allowed the *stratêgos* to concentrate on honing the riders' specifically military techniques, and in teaching them to execute familiar actions with the greater speed and precision demanded by battlefield conditions, such as mounting swiftly with the encumbrance of more complete arms and armour than the men may have been accustomed to. The manuals are quite detailed regarding some of these exercises. One exercise recommended by Emperor Leo was follows:

> *In shooting from horseback [a horseman should practice] to swiftly loose one or two arrows, and then to put the strung bow away in the case, if it is wide, or otherwise in another half case, to which it fits in a suitable manner. Then he should take up the lance resting on his shoulder, and with the strung bow in its case, brandish the lance. Then [he should] quickly replace it on his shoulder, taking hold of the bow.*

Archery was to be mastered shooting in all directions at all speeds up to the gallop. The lancers were trained in the technique of protecting their mounts' heads and throats with their shields as they passed at a collected canter through the field of hostile archery.

A solitary cavalryman was both ineffective and vulnerable, so the critical training once the troops were assembled was to acquaint them, or re-acquaint them, with the need for discipline and restraint in their riding in order to maintain a cohesive unit. As well as forming the equivalent of the infantry's *kontouvernion*, a pair of men known as 'spear companions' was also the smallest unit of operations for the battlefield. They were to stay together under all circumstances. Recognition of the unit banner and the need to rally to it as the default course of action were also drilled to be second nature.

BELOW LEFT
The optimum method for horse archers to attack a static formation. The horsemen can shoot all along the arc of attack, which means that their targets receive missiles from multiple directions, often onto their unshielded side. The archer at the far left is executing the famous, ancient Parthian shot, shooting backward whilst riding away, which Roman horse archers of this period were expected to master as well as any other. The diagram shows how this technique can be used in coordination with a frontal assault by heavy cavalry.

BELOW
Another technique for combined cavalry assault. The horse archers shoot over the heads of the *katafraktoi*, aiming to disorder the enemy ranks prior to the heavy cavalry's impact, and then continue to harass the surrounding units using the Parthian shot while turning away, thereby reducing their capacity to reinforce the area struck by the *katafraktoi*.

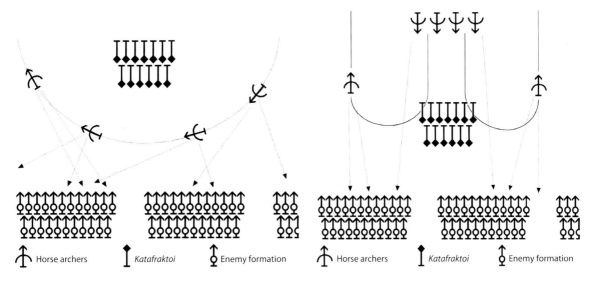

Horse archers   *Katafraktoi*   Enemy formation   Horse archers   *Katafraktoi*   Enemy formation

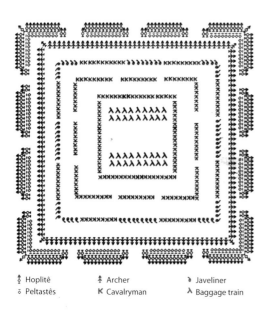

‡ Hoplitē   ‡ Archer   ⅃ Javeliner
ŏ Peltastēs   K Cavalryman   ⅄ Baggage train

Schematic diagram of the square formation from an eleventh-century manuscript. The infantry square forms a human fortification that serves as a base for cavalry operations; they may sally out through any of the intervals.

This twelfth- to thirteenth-century relief of hunters (the other half is shown on page 29) is displayed in the Islamic Museum, Istanbul, but several features, primarily the straight, tapering swords and long-stirrup riding style, make it plain that the men are not Turks. Rather, they are Romans, or else Armenians, perhaps from Kilikia. (Author's photograph)

Commands could be transmitted by various means, and the troops had to be accustomed to recognizing and responding to these in all circumstances. Any substantial group of riders in motion created a significant noise, so verbal commands would only have been used when a unit was immobile. The manuals suggest that there were several different sorts of wind instruments used to deliver different orders. If the men were to move off, a command was given verbally (*Kineson*, 'March' or *Exelte*, 'Head out'), by means of a dip of the standard or by sounding one sort of horn. When a halt was required, the order might be given by striking a shield with a weapon or by means of a trumpet (*voukina*).

Training and exercises did not cease when the expeditionary force took to the road. Manoeuvres were conducted across all sorts of terrain. Leo was more demanding than his predecessors, urging his troops to master operating in more rugged areas. As with the infantry, these exercises included mock battles with practice weapons – spears and arrows without points, and sticks in place of swords and maces. It is possible that the Roman army's habit of holding practice battles may well have contributed to the development of the European tournament. One of the earliest recorded tournaments was an encounter at Antioch between members of the imperial court and the Franco-Norman retinue of the ruler of the Crusader Principality of Antioch, in 1137. Holding such practice battles as public entertainments became quite popular in the capital later in the twelfth century.

APPEARANCE

The degree to which the earlier Roman army wore anything resembling uniform remains a matter of fierce debate. The evidence for the tenth century does not resolve the issue, for the military manuals have little specific to say about the dress of the troops, but by supplementing them with detail derived from other sources some confident conclusions can be drawn. The *Stratêgikon* had recommended 'Avar' garments for the cavalry, which can be taken to mean tunics split in the centre, a feature already shown in the art of Late Antiquity. The manuals are unanimous in recommending that military garments were to hang no lower than the knee, in the manner of labouring men, and in contrast to the dominant civilian fashion for men of higher status to wear tunics to the ankle. The manuals stress that the appearance of the troops should be neat and well presented, observing that, just as in more recent armies, these qualities are bound up inevitably with morale, and hence combat effectiveness. Beyond these considerations, the sources do not clearly suggest a high degree of uniformity in the dress of soldiers. It is likely that it depended upon how much centralized or centrally coordinated supply could be mobilized by the officer organizing a unit. Since the times of the earlier empire there had been intricate rules that governed clothing for civilian men, especially in the court context, and these had increased over the centuries. The effect of these rules was to create blocks of uniform colour and style whenever men of similar rank were gathered together. Hence, it is most likely there was a conspicuous division between provincial thematic units and metropolitan tagmatic corps, with the former tending to diversity, and the latter to uniformity following the example set at court, particularly in view of their occasional involvement in imperial ceremonies.

Hunting has always been one of the most common ways in which a man of the equestrian fraternity maintained his skills when not committed to the battlefield. Hunting lions with hand weapons had a special kudos in the literature and art of Rômania, just as it did in al-Islamiyya. (Author's photograph)

In addition to fine details of horse furniture, this eleventh-century ivory in the Victoria and Albert Museum shows a practice that is rarely depicted, but which must, in fact, have been the norm – that of hanging the shield from a shoulder strap. (Author's photograph)

The popularly accepted image of tunics in the Eastern Roman Empire is rather stuck in a Late Antique time warp. By the tenth century much had changed. Rather than the shapeless 'Coptic' sacks of Old Rome, a man of Constantinople commonly wore an *esôforion* (shirt) and a *roukhon* (outer tunic) tailored and fitted in quite a sophisticated manner. The neckline was round and close fitting, opening down from the left side of the neck in a style that went back to ancient Persia, and the *esôforion* was finished with a low collar fastened with a small button. The sleeves extended fully over the wrist; the cuffs were close fitting and sometimes had a short opening fastened even more tightly to the wrist with a single button. *Esôforia* were made of linen and were either white or, less often, in pastel shades. Ordinary *roukha* were made of wool or heavier linen. Rich reds and blues predominate in pictorial sources, reflecting the primacy of *kirmis* and indigo dyes.

The late-Roman writer Vegetius had recommended that the 'Pannonian' hat should be worn by soldiers when they were not wearing helmets. The hat of cylindrical appearance which is commonly associated with this term was still in use in the tenth to twelfth century, and more detailed representations of this era show that it was not a true *pyxis* (pillbox) shape but rather a deep round-ended cylinder with the closed end on the head and the open end turned up outside to conceal the crown. A variety of other hats were popular through the period, although none of these had specifically military associations. Doubtless, the thick felt caps which served as helmet linings and turban bases were worn much of the time by troops, as, indeed, must the turbans wrapped directly on the head that were common to civilian fashion.

A number of other fashions known from civilian contexts had military utility as well. The old Roman disdain for the barbarians' trousers had taken on a new lease of life with the adoption of the Persian habit of wearing leggings suspended from the trouser-cord over lighter breeches. By the tenth century, even in civilian use, the leggings could be padded with wool, cotton or even silk floss. This was simply for protection from the cold for civilians, but it would be even more valuable as a supplement to leg protection for soldiers. The likelihood of such leggings, which were originally called *kampotouva* or 'field-hose', being in common military use is confirmed by the fact that even the emperor would wear them as part of his military regalia from time to time. Pictures indicate that *kampotouva* were normally quilted in a diamond pattern, sometimes with a small motif in the middle of each.

Not surprisingly, the manuals give more attention to the troops' footwear than any other aspect of clothing – for nothing, short of starvation, is more damaging to an army on campaign than poor footwear. The fact that cavalry were not expected to travel any great distance on foot meant that the discussion focused mainly on the infantry, but the fact that cavalrymen generally had greater status and wealth must have resulted in them having footwear at least as good as anything the foot soldiers possessed. From as early as the sixth century there is a surviving example of what is unmistakably a riding boot – calf-length with a stiff flap projecting up at the front to cover the kneecap. From the eleventh century there are depictions of softer thigh boots tied up to the trouser cord. These were probably invented within the empire somewhat earlier, via a ready fusion of boots with the *kampotouva* mentioned above. The ancient term *hypodimata* is used for thigh boots, while boots below the knee were *mouzakia*. Shoes *(sandalia* and *tzervoulia)* are mentioned as a poor substitute for the infantry and were probably only ever seen on the servants of the cavalry arm. The standard colours in men's footwear were, just as today, natural tan through brown and black, with a few other colours (red, orange, blue and green) being restricted by law to particular high court ranks. The archaeology of the late antique cemeteries of Egypt shows that Near Eastern footwear technology was far ahead of that of Europe. Patterns much like many still in use today were employed, and more substantial shoes and boots had thick, multi-layered soles.

When dressed for battle, the overall appearance of the troops was determined by the padded coats that formed the most extensive protection for the horse archers (*zava* or *kavadion*) and were a surcoat for the more heavily armoured cavalry (*epilôrikion*). Given their construction, and the fact that the manuals are very detailed about their form, they were probably a specialized item more commonly supplied by central arrangement, and therefore likely to be more uniform in their appearance, perhaps, like the tunics, of a common colour by unit. In the latter part of the period there are hints that the *epilôrikia* of the more eminent and wealthy cavaliers could be brightly coloured, if not patterned, or decorated with quasi-heraldic emblems, anticipating the appearance of later Western knights. Towards the end of the civil war of 1080–81 Alexios I Komnênos requisitioned silk civilian clothing to cover up a deficit in his troops' armour. His (Roman) opponents presumably were not expected to be surprised to see such opulent fabrics on the battlefield. The eponymous hero of the romance *Digenis Akritas*, first written down around the turn of the twelfth century, is described as wearing an *epilôrikion* embroidered with a gryphon. Ample pictorial sources give the common quilting patterns used on these garments. They were normally vertical linear compartments cross-quilted in various ways to forestall slippage of the cotton wadding, but there are hints that a parade version of the surcoat (*gounion*) might have been quilted in more decorative arabesque patterns.

Officers were set apart by wearing a cloth sash tied around the chest, called a *pektorarion*. These sashes must have been colour-coded for different

Another outstanding ivory in the Victoria and Albert Museum illustrates exceptional details of tack, and fine ornamental saddle pad. This may have been used for stirrupless training, for normally the breast and rump straps shown here were secured to the saddle rather than the pad. (Author's photograph)

ranks, but unfortunately there is no record of the precise correlations, which must have been either dictated by custom or set ad hoc in a given expeditionary army.

One aspect of uniformity is explicitly recommended in the manuals, and that is that all the shields of each unit be painted the same. In addition, although not mentioned in the literature, pictorial sources quite often show similarities between the way the shields are painted and the patterning on the main field of the common form of banner. So it is possible that they were also coordinated, thus helping to further cement the cohesion of the company in battle.

One very conspicuous aspect of the troops' appearance stems from the admonition that idle time in camp was to be occupied in keeping arms and armour polished. Besides forestalling the 'devil's work', well-maintained kit, like the clothing mentioned above, was both an expression of, and a factor in, good morale.

EQUIPMENT

Although the rider's dress and equipment is characterized by antiquarian stylization, other evidence confirms that the horse furniture shown on the Barberini Ivory is a good indication of how ornamental the best middle Byzantine era could be. (Picture courtesy Marie Lan-Nguyen)

As the elite wing of the army and the one expected to bear the brunt of the fighting in most battles, the authorities always expected the cavalry to have more and better equipment than the infantry. The degree to which such expectations were met is hard to assess, especially when a major part of the mounted arm was composed of *strateioumenoi* who supplied their own kit to the best of their financial ability. Economic factors could be just as stringent on centralized supply as well; we know that Alexios Komnênos requisitioned civilian clothing to fake surcoats for his horsemen towards the end of the civil war that brought him to power.

In theory, the three subdivisions of the cavalry, the archers, the *khoursôres*, and the *katafraktoi* were characterized by their armour in particular, although in practice such divisions were undoubtedly blurred.

With mobility paramount, the basic kit of the archers was a padded coat *(kavadion)* made, according to Emperor Nikêforos, of cotton padding covered with raw silk and 'as thick as may be stitched', that is, perhaps as much as five centimetres. The sleeves of these coats were full length, but mobility being optimised by an opening to pass the arms, either in the elbow according to the *Syllogê Taktikôn* and Leo's *Taktika,* or in the armpit according to the two *Nikêforoi*, with the empty part of the sleeve being fastened back behind the shoulder. Fôkas gives the very useful information that part of the skirt of the archers' coats was to cover some of the horse's rump, thus showing that they must have been made in the three-panelled form known from Caucasian archaeological finds. The archer might wear a simple *klivanion* of lamellae or a scale shirt over his coat, but only

covering his chest and back without the encumbrance of solid sleeves or skirts. He could also have a light helm, probably with a padded neck guard. Leo was adamant that they ought not to carry shields on account of the obstruction they could cause to shooting flexibility. The archers were not entirely helpless if they could not avoid a close-quarters clash, for they did carry a sword, generally the slightly curved, single-edged *paramêrion* either hung from a belt or a shoulder strap. Their main armament was, of course, the bow, a composite recurve with a smooth profile, rather than the Central Asian style with 'ears', carried strung in a case on the left side. The power of these bows was to be tailored to the capacity of the men rather than their being forced to work up to a higher draw weight. They carried 30 to 40 arrows at a time, contained point outermost in a cylindrical quiver hung from the belt. The point-up method allows for the most efficient loading onto the bow, but does have its dangers, as illustrated by the death of Emperor Iôannês (II) Komnênos from septicaemia as a result of having accidentally pierced his hand on one of his arrowheads. Arrows for military use carried a variety of heads from the general purpose, smooth, conical pile to heavy, multifaceted, armour-piercing bodkins. Archers carried lighter, bladed and barbed heads for hunting as well. The ubiquitous fletching method for horse archery arrows is four flights framing the nock, allowing the arrow to be nocked either way simply by touch. Flights were a symmetrical crescent shape and quite small by modern, or, indeed, Western medieval standards.

As the *koursôres* bore the burden of hand-to-hand combat, the aim was for them to have reasonably complete armour, and this must have varied considerably. At the bottom end, there must have been some who were little better-supplied than the archers, while Leo acknowledges that at the top end were, indeed, *katafraktoi*. Mail was the time-honoured default armour. Leo echoes the *Stratêgikon* by describing the cavalry *lôrikion alusidôton* as extending to the ankles. Some modern commentators have doubted this, but it is a functional arrangement presaging the European knight's mail hose, and supported by the statement that these *lôrikia* should have 'thongs and rings allowing the skirts to be caught up', that is to say, bound to the legs while riding and tied back up to the belt to facilitate walking. A mail shirt could be

EQUIPMENT

Just as with the infantry, the cavalry of the enduring Roman Empire had three classes of troops whose equipment reflected the nature, proximity and duration of the contact they were expected to have with the enemy. The lightest cavalryman was the archer (**1**). While he was equipped with a sword, usually the slightly curved *paramêrion*, and sometimes (although Leo advised against it) with a small buckler, his primary armament was his bow. His closest contact was only expected to be returning arrows, hence his protective gear was light. At the lowest end it comprised a heavy turban over a thick cap and a padded *kavadion* (coat) made of cotton wadding in a raw silk cover 'as thick as may be stitched', as Fôkas puts it. The general's detailed description tells us that that such coats must have been made in the same manner as a surviving civilian example with the skirt in three panels so that when mounted the front two covered the man's thighs and the rear afforded some protection to the horse. The sleeves, although likely to be functional for general wear, had openings either at the elbows (according to Leo) or in the armpits (according to Nikêforos Fôkas) through which the arms were placed to allow freedom of movement while in combat. The empty lower portion was fastened back to the shoulder to get it out of the way. In a particularly well-supplied army, an archer might have a light helm with a padded neckguard, and a lamellar *klivanion* covering only his chest and back. The *koursôres* were medium troops who had the most flexible and far-ranging role (**2**). They were expected to engage in hand-to-hand combat, but normally only with other medium to light cavalry or with small or disordered groups of infantry. Thus, they needed armour with a good level of protection, but not so heavy or cumbersome as to tire the horses during their often quite extended excursions. Over a padded *zava*, which could be either a coat or a pullover, the *koursôr* would wear a *lôrikion koinon* or *alusidôton* (mail shirt) or a *lôrikion folidôton* (a shirt of scales). The mail hood had been in use in the Roman army since at least the beginning of the seventh century. Alternatively, the helm would have had an attached mail skirt to guard his neck, but padding or leather scales were less costly options. He carried a round shield of about 80cm in diameter as his first line of defence. His initial weapons were a 2.9m lance, which Leo suggests could be worn slung across the back if he were also carrying projectile weapons, a baldric-hung sword of either type, and probably a mace or two holstered on his saddle. The *katafraktos* (**3**) was the tank of his day. The sheer weight of kit carried by this man and his horse meant that they were only used over the shortest distances and against the hardest and most critical targets. The full range of components of his armour according to the rationalised scheme of Nikêforos Fôkas can be seen on page 55, but here you can see the overall appearance of a fully equipped trooper with virtually all the hard gear hidden by his *epilôrikion*, which was a padded coat of the same substance as the archer's *kavadion* described above. All cavalry shields were round through most of this period, until an adoption of Western practice introduced kite shields to the heavy cavalry later in the twelfth century. On his person, the *katafraktos* carried one of each type of sword, *spathion* and *paramêrion*, along with up to three maces, two holstered on his saddle and the third in the hand if he was not commencing the engagement armed with the *kontarion* lance.

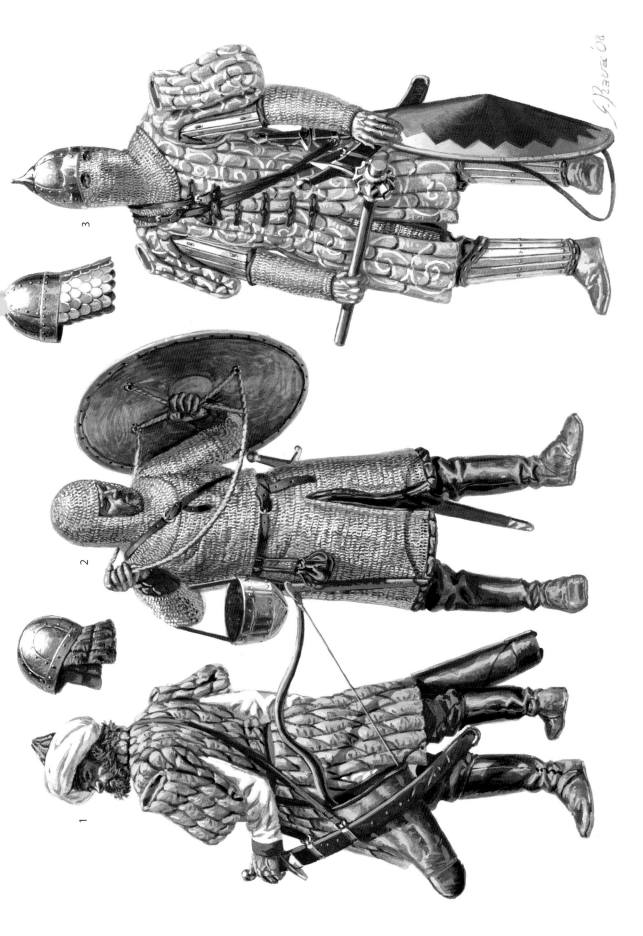

supplemented by a lamellar *klivanion* and limb pieces thus putting the man into the class of *katafraktos*. Scale (*lôrikion folidôton*) was a widespread alternative to mail. Scale armours could range from a simple breast and back, like the minimal *klivanion*, to a full shirt with sleeves and divided skirts like mail. Helms were to be fitted with a mail skirt, which Leo advised should cover all of the the face but for the eyes. Fôkas elaborated this for his *katafraktoi* by saying that the mail skirt should be double layered. Additional limb armour was to be used wherever possible. As well as protection for the forearms (*kheiropsella*) and lower legs (*podopsella*), upper sleeves attached to the *klivanion* were all made of splinted construction; the latter is often mistaken for the ancient and long-abandoned *pteruges* in mildly stylized middle Byzantine era pictures. Solid lower leg defences (*khalkotouva*) were still in use, while later, upper arm pieces fitted to the *klivanion* and skirts could be made of scales or inverted lamellae.

Koursôres and *katafraktoi* were further protected by carrying a shield. Originally this was round, with the longer forms restricted to infantry, but in the twelfth century the percolation of Western practices into the army meant that the kite shield was adopted by heavier cavalry as well. Round shields (*skoutaria*) could be domed or conical in section, and up to 90cm in diameter according to the manuals, although those shown in art tend to be smaller, a more practical 75–80cm. Such shields were fitted with a pair of rope or leather handles attached separately at each end to rings fixed into the body of the shield. In combat on foot they were gripped in the fist like a buckler, but on horseback they were suspended from a shoulder strap and probably stabilized by threading the arm through one loop to have it sit in the crook of the elbow. It seems clear that these shields were commonly built on a base of cane or wickerwork like the practice shields mentioned by Vegetius.

The widest range of armament was available to these troops, and they would often be carrying multiple weapons, in part because weapons do break, but all the more because a horseman can hardly dismount in the midst of battle to recover a dropped weapon or re-arm. Lances seem oddly short to anyone familiar with later medieval European practice – no longer than the shorter infantry spear, about 2.5m, but it is clear that the lance was not considered to be so important as a cavalry weapon. Swords existed in two primary forms: the straight, double-edged *spathion* and the slightly curved, single-edged *paramêrion*. These swords could be hung either from a shoulder strap (baldric) or waist belt. In the case of the *spathion*, the choice of suspension method determined how the sword hung. The attachment points for a baldric were opposite each other on either side of the scabbard as with the old *gladius*, and so the weapon hung vertically by the leg. The attachments for the belt-hung (*zôstikion*) *spathion* were on the same side of the scabbard, and therefore the sword hung close to horizontal. Hanging points for the *paramêrion* were the same for either suspension method, on the same side of the scabbard, and hence the sword hung close to horizontal 'beside the thigh', a literal translation of the name. Troopers wearing the more flexible sorts of armour, archers in their *kavadia* or *koursôres* in *lôrikia alusidôta*, could use either belt or baldric suspension for their swords. Horsemen clad in lamellar or the more comprehensive form of *lôrikion folidôton* used shoulder straps as it was impractical to put a belt on or under such armour. Fôkas wanted his *katafraktoi* to carry one of each sort of sword, an entirely practical arrangement as the hilts of the vertically hanging *spathion* and the horizontally hanging *paramêrion* are well separated and one can draw either readily.

The mace was the cavalryman's weapon par excellence. Their heads are well represented in archaeology and sometimes in art. Globular forms predominate, mostly with triangular spikes of various sizes, but flanged styles also occur. In addition to the familiar arrangement of an iron head on a wooden shaft, the tenth century had already seen an innovation visible later in the West with certain maces, called *sideroravdion* and *spathovaklion*, being made with iron shafts fitted with a guard and hilt like a sword. These were even part of the regalia of certain grades of courtier. In addition to mentioning the wholly iron maces, the twelfth-century Arab writer Al-Tartusi says that some of the more common sorts could be highly ornamental with the wooden handle wrapped in fine leather with painted decoration. Axes were less favoured but still used from horseback. The main blade on battle axes varied from somewhat flared to a full, almost semicircular crescent like the later eastern *tabar*. The secondary fitting could be the same, or else could consist of a hammerhead, a spike or a blade like a spear point.

Nikêforos Fôkas seems to have made a concerted effort to increase the number of *katafraktoi* in his army. Some have suggested that he invented a new form of *katafraktos*, but a more careful comparison between him and the preceding sources shows that what Fôkas in fact did was to define a somewhat pared down and modular system for the body armour which would have made these troops cheaper and simpler to equip, at the cost of certain specific reductions in their defences. Thus, while a Leonine *katafraktos* would have strapped his lamellar and upper sleeves on over a full padded garment and mail shirt, making him more burdened and over-armoured in the chest area, but covering the chinks (armpits, elbows and so on), the Nikêforian *katafraktos* donned a *klivanion* directly over a hip-length, short-sleeved arming jacket (*zoupa*), then attached splinted upper sleeves, and padded skirts and padded lower sleeves all faced with mail. Having so much less mail represented a great labour and cost saving, but left areas like the armpits and elbow joints much less protected. This is a process precisely paralleled in European armour of the later fourteenth and early fifteenth centuries; perhaps the Romans also had the

Detail of a jug depicting the empire's most effective new enemy of the eleventh century – Seljuk Turks. Like so many, they were originally nomadic herders from Central Asia who tied their children onto the backs of goats to acclimatize themselves to riding from the earliest age. (Photo courtesy of Steven Baker.)

idea of applying the mail facings to the armpits and elbows of the arming jacket, just as the Westerners did. In any case, Fôkas' innovation may have made *katafraktoi* more common that they had been hitherto, and almost certainly more common than the curiously low numbers that have been estimated by some scholars – little more than 500 for the entire empire.

Armour construction

Archaeological remains of helms in this period are depressingly rare, and the artistic conventions of the time also mean that they were seldom illustrated. Such evidence there is, however, does paint a picture largely of developmental continuity with late antiquity. Most prevalent is a simplified form of the five-piece ridge helm known primarily from several fourth-century examples found at Intercisa in Germany. The barbarian spangenhelm also continued in

EQUIPMENT: THE NIKÊFORIAN *KATAFRAKTOS* AND BEYOND

The Roman *katafraktos* of the tenth to twelfth centuries was the equivalent of the modern main battle tank. It would be several hundred years before anyone in the West took to the battlefield so well protected. The detailed description given by General (later Emperor) Nikêforos Fôkas in the *Composition on Warfare* (traditionally known by its Latinized title *Praecepta Militaria*) represents an outstanding compromise between protection, minimal encumbrance and weight, and ease of supply. The arming sequence followed here is from an earlier manual which sought to ensure that the donning of each piece of armour was not obstructed by any previous piece, and that a man could arm himself unaided as much as possible. (**1**) First was the *peristhêthidion* or *zoupa*, a padded jacket with short sleeves, which closely matched the size and form of the cuirass that was to go over it. Sources show these could be either button-up or pull-over types. Then came the *podopsella* or greaves (**1A**). These are most likely to have been splinted, although there are some indications that, at least in the latter part of the period, they could be solid tubes. Next came the *kremasmata*, a pair of padded skirts faced with mail (**2A**). How these, and other items, were attached is unknown, but a practical method in keeping with known practices of the region would be to lace them to the bottom of the *zoupa*. *Kremasmata* were later made of scales (**2B**) or inverted lamellae (**2C**). The *klivanion* was next (**3**). Lamellae was known, but was of marginal importance, in the early imperial Roman army. When it returned, probably in the later eighth century, its potential was rapidly realized, and Byzantine artisans introduced a series of technological refinements unique to the Eastern Roman Empire which made it cheaper and more serviceable. The pattern shown here was the second generation of those innovations, which has rows of plates fixed to a leather backing by riveting top and bottom before hanging by the traditional laces. The precise method by which the *klivanion* was secured is unknown, but the author's experiments show that a poncho arrangement fastened with straps and buckles at the sides is viable, although it does require assistance at both ends of the arming process. After this came the *manikellia*; the upper sleeves were originally also splinted (**4A**), which is why in the stylization of religious art they could pass for the antique Roman *pteruges*. Initially they were most probably laced directly to the *klivanion*, but as the armouring progressed a shaped shoulder-piece was fitted (**4C/4D**). Like the *kremasmata*, later *manikellia* could be of scales (**4B**) or inverted lamellae (**4D**). Next would normally come the helmet (**5**). Fôkas decrees that the mail skirt hanging from the helm should be two layers thick and cover everything but the eyes. All the body armour was enclosed in an *epilôrikion*, a padded surcoat probably identical in form to the *kavadion* worn by the archers (see plate [D] on page 35). Finally, when everything else was buckled, laced and buttoned, the *kheiropsella* or forearm defences (**6**) were put on. The general suggests that they should be made, like the *kremasmata*, of mail laid over padding. Again, these were probably laced to the sleeves of the *zoupa*, a point at which the trooper would need some assistance, either from his 'spear companion' or the groom they shared. As equipment was usually personally acquired by better financed troopers, it was probably quite common for a *katafraktos* to wear his *klivanion* over a full *zava* and *lôrikion* like the *koursôr* of plate [D] on page 35, rather than the discrete mail-faced pieces, thereby gaining additional protection, especially for vulnerable places like the armpits. The sources also mention mailed *kheiromanikia*, or gloves. On his person, the *katafraktos* carried two swords hung from shoulder straps: a straight, double-edged *spathion*, and a slightly curved, single-edged *paramêrion*. He had two maces in holsters on either side of the front of his saddle to fall back on, and would commence a sally with either a spear, mace or axe in hand.

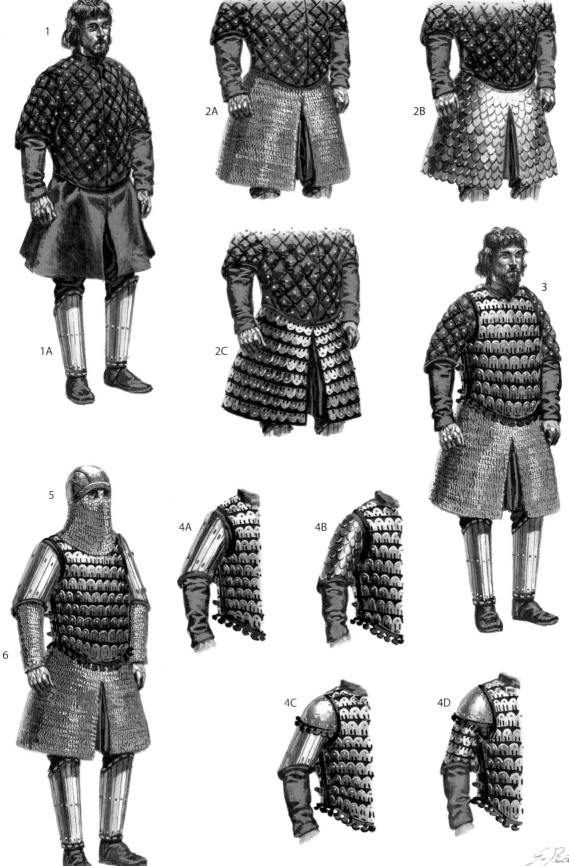

use, now, like the ridge helms, bereft of cheek plates. The taller, more pointed form of spangenhelm, commonly known as 'Caucasian' due to the numerous tenth- to eleventh-century examples found in Russia and the Ukraine, was also probably in use from the beginning of the period, although examples are not found in East Roman art until the eleventh century. The unique survival known as the Yasenovo helm attributed to the ninth or tenth century is a quite different construction. Whether it is genuinely an innovation is uncertain, though. The reinforcing bands across the crown hark back to the modifications made to legionary helmets in the early third century to counter the power of the Dacian *falx*, but may just be a pragmatic response to a similar threat. Pictures in the illustrated manuscript of the chronicle of Skylitzes show that forms like the Yasenovo helm must have been almost as widespread as the ridge helm. In the twelfth century we seem to see some innovations coming in, although whether they arise within the empire, or are imported very rapidly from neighbours, or merely begin to be illustrated belatedly is not clear. One is the appearance of early forms of 'kettle hat' – one-piece helms with a slight brim. The manifest long-term collective memory of the Roman army may mean that this was a revival based upon remembered

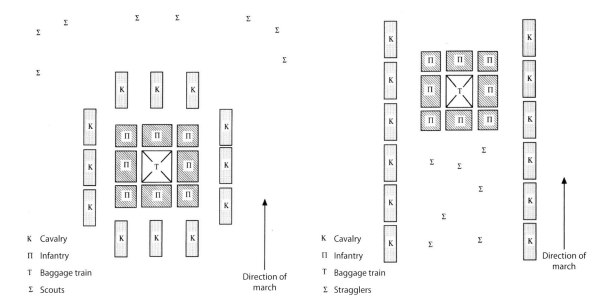

K	Cavalry
Π	Infantry
T	Baggage train
Σ	Scouts

Direction of march

K	Cavalry
Π	Infantry
T	Baggage train
Σ	Stragglers

Direction of march

forms, or even that brimmed forms had never fallen completely out of use. The other innovation might also be a revival of a remembered ancient form. The Phrygian cap-style helm swept the Mediterranean in the twelfth century with no regard for cultural boundaries.

All these might be worn plain, or over a separate hood of mail, known in the Roman Empire since Late Antiquity, but they would often carry some form of attached neck protection. The ridge helms seem to have commonly borne a padded skirt at least. The quilting patterns shown on these are often suggestive of *pteruges*, and it is possible that leather *pteruges* may sometimes have been used as a low-grade substitute. Phrygian cap helms also show these forms of neck protection at times. The surviving Caucasian helms seem to have routinely carried a mail skirt, either linked on through holes punched in the rim, as with some of the early medieval European spangenhelms, or attached by a more sophisticated method whereby the edge was rolled

ABOVE LEFT
The basic marching formation whereby the cavalry in four units screens the faces of the infantry and baggage train.

ABOVE RIGHT
A marching formation for more difficult circumstances. The horsemen have formed two long lines to protect the sides of the foot soldiers and baggage train, extending back to cover stragglers such as the wounded following an unsuccessful battle.

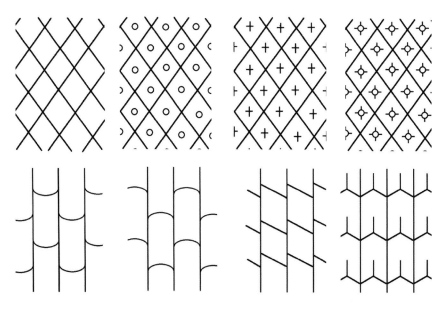

Quilted military garments are shown in remarkable detail in pictorial sources, giving a good insight into the range of methods used. The diamond patterns were used for the jackets worn under more solid armour. The more intricate diamond-with-motif could be used for the parade coats of officers and elite units, and are sometimes seen on leggings. Long garments such as *kavadia* and *epilôrikia* usually employed patterns based upon vertical panels. There are hints that very opulent *epilôrikia* might be quilted in arabesques.

41

into a tube, then cut into a comb, with the mail strung on a wire threaded through the comb. This suspension system is also found on the Yasenovo helm. Illustrations of the early brimmed helms also show mail hangings, but without any indication as to how they were attached.

Lamellar (*klivanion*) was another armour known to the early imperial Roman army, but it seems to have fallen out of use amidst the tribulations of the fall of the West. By the beginning of the tenth century it had returned, and thereafter rapidly undergoes a series of technological refinements which produce distinctively Byzantine types which do not seem to have been known to its neighbours or clients. The widespread form with which the early Romans were acquainted was entirely laced. The tenth-century innovations start to make it into something like an inside-out brigandine, initially with rows of plates laced, then riveted, to a leather backing before the rows were suspended. The vast harm done to the economy and industrial base of the empire by the Fourth Crusade spelled the end for lamellar in the Roman army.

Horse equipment

Sources for horse furniture in the middle Byzantine period are unfortunately confined to a relatively small number of sometimes stylized pictures, and for equine military equipment are confined solely to literary references, so there is no certainty about the fine details. In practice there is little potential for functional variety in bridles, and the only differences shown in the pictures is the presence or otherwise of a nose band. There are a few illustrations of curbed bits, but the majority show no distinctive features and must be

F   **HORSE EQUIPMENT**

The form of much horse equipment is remarkably consistent across time and cultures. Eastern equestrian practice, even in the military, never embraced the Western chivalric enthusiasm for the energy and aggression of the stallion, preferring to use geldings and mares. One result of this was that less brutal methods were required to control mounts than were often used in the West. While curb bits (**2**) were in use, variants of the snaffle (**1**) predominated. Bridles appear scarcely to differ from those commonly in use today. The tack of wealthier riders would provide avenues for display of status, of course, with bridle straps being decorated with metal plaques, and ornamental roundels covering the junction points. Saddles of the Central Asian form with low pommel and cantle prevail across the period. They were made in four pieces – the two arches for the pommel and cantle, and the side bars curved in two dimensions to match the average horse's back and thick in the middle to form the seat (**3**). Basic saddles were used as is, with the rider sitting directly on the wood, while better models had a layer of upholstery to ease the discomfort. Later in the twelfth century, heavy cavalry troops who did not need the flexibility to use archery began to adopt the higher pommel and cantle saddles in use amongst Western knights. In addition to the girths, saddles were normally fitted with a breast and rump strap (**4**). These could be plain leather, but again might be a site for status display. Even plain ones could have a few pendant straps, while the most ornamental could have multiple figured metal roundels similar to the horse brasses of modern times. Leo recommended that every trooper had a saddlebag or bags (**5**) containing three days' rations as a precaution against the misadventure of being separated from his unit. The mounts of the *katafraktoi* who were expected to inflict frontal attacks on infantry formations were equipped with iron headpieces and their chests and necks protected by *klivania* of ox-hide lamellar, or coverings of laminated felt (**6**). The lack of surviving examples and of good depictions leaves only guesswork for the form of middle Byzantine era headpieces. General Near Eastern and Central Asian practices tended to make them more encompassing than later Western *chamfrons* generally were. Leather lamellar gained no benefit from the technological refinements pioneered in Constantinople for human armour and that applied to metal and horn forms, and so this element probably retained the elementary form of the ubiquitous hanging lamellar construction with plates laced together horizontally and then the rows suspended. Also shown is a typical stirrup (**7**).

Although the manuals mention wagons, it is clear that very often the entire army's supplies were carried on mules, for much of the Balkans in particular had very poor roads. This is a detail from an eleventh-century manuscript picture showing mules with their packsaddles. In camp, such saddles were commonly used as seats, the only furniture an ordinary soldier, or common traveller, had available. (Esphigmenou Monastery, Mt Athos)

presumed to be the snaffle type. Some decoration could be applied to bridles, most conspicuously ornamental roundels on the intersections of the pieces, and occasionally on the centre of the brow band. Saddles had a low pommel and cantle and no distinctive features in the surviving sources. Later in the twelfth century, the adoption of Western methods resulted in the use of the high cantle and pommel knightly saddle by the heavier troops. Besides the essential girth, saddles were further stabilized by straps around the breast and rump. These could be fitted with a variable number of short pendants, either plain straps or terminating in decorative roundels. In terms of military equipment, the sources mention head defences and breast armour, although rump protection does not seem to have been as common. We must assume that the headpieces were more solid than the leather ones that survive from the early imperial period, but we have no evidence regarding their precise form. There is more information about the other armour used for the horses. Ideally the chest and neck pieces were composed of lamellae made of ox hide. The secondary option was heavy, laminated felt. A final item of horse armour which period sources attribute exclusively to the Romans is a shoe covering the entirety of the underside of the hoof to protect the animal from caltrops, a descendent of the tied-on horseshoes of the early imperial era.

ON CAMPAIGN

The first stage of any military campaign is mobilization. When the emperor himself was to participate this was signalled by the display of a sword, mail shirt and shield hung on the outside of the Khalkê Gate of the Walls of Theodosios. Notice was sent to the *stratêgoi* or *doukes* of the regions in which the campaign was to be waged or through which it would pass so that they could commence

The thumb draw is the horseman's form of archery par excellence. Sources like this fragment of mosaic from the Great Palace in Constantinople show that the Romans adopted the method in Late Antiquity. It also shows some good detail of the type of bow in use. (Author's photograph)

The fresco of the Forty Martyrs of Sevastê in the Dovecote Church at Çavusin in Kappadokhia shows both infantry and cavalry. The horsemen are armed with *kontaria* and protected by a mixture of lamellar and scale armour. (Photo courtesy of Steven Lowe)

their preparations for involvement or contribution. The primary preparations were the gathering of supplies (grain, edible livestock and other foods), the amassing of equipment (arms, armour, saddlery, tents, wagons and so on), the requisitioning of additional mounts and beasts of burden, and the summoning of the *strateioumenoi* from their farms.

The cavalry equivalent of the infantry *kontouvernion* (and probably called the same) was a pair of horsemen with a manservant/groom who shared a tent. Both round pavilions and rectangular tents were in use, and while it is clear enough that the former were probably the norm for an infantry file, it is hard to say whether one sort or the other was preferred for a cavalry mess. The greater affluence which typified cavalry troops may have meant that they could indulge themselves in such luxuries as campbeds, which are mentioned in routinely negative terms in the sources, in preference to the bedrolls of less well-off soldiers. *Strateioumenoi* also seem, at least at times, to have brought some provisions with them when they mobilized, and if they were campaigning not too far from home might have been able to restock from that source. If not, they were obliged to fall back on the basic fare of the mass of the army. Various grains formed the basis of campaign rations. They were initially carried both in prepared form and as flour. The main preparation of grain was hardtack, called *paximata* or *paximadion*. This was coarse, double-baked bread. The simplest form was made from grain alone, but better types could include dried fruits and meats. More complex prepared rations are also described in the sources composed of a mixture of vegetables, nuts, seeds and honey. A marginal note in one tenth-century siegecraft manual describes a ration prepared from roasted sesame, honey, oil, almonds and squill, an astringently flavoured vegetable. Trials by members of the Hetaireia Palatiou confirm the source's claim that such food was 'good also for campaigning, for it is sweet and filling and does not induce thirst.' A basic hot meal could be made from milled millet cooked up as a form of porridge. In richer seasons, troops might have the benefit of a common peasant staple still eaten today, *trakhanas*. This is made of cracked wheat mixed with yoghurt, and was formed into balls or small loaves and left to dry in the sun. Like this it could keep for long periods and was boiled into a soup or stew to be eaten, often garnished with chunks of feta cheese. Well-planned expeditions doubtless set off with supplies of preserved meat as well. Fresh supplies were purchased, requisitioned or foraged as the campaign progressed. Mealtimes were announced in camp by trumpet, although in the sources there are differing opinions about how many meals there should be and when. In practice, set meals were probably a light breakfast and a dinner, with anything in between being an ad hoc affair arranged around whatever was the business of the time.

On the road various formations were adopted depending upon the composition of the army and circumstances. Whether from city or camp, the cavalry would move off first so their activities would not be obstructed by the less mobile infantry and baggage train. Commonly thereafter, where space allowed, the horsemen would divide into four to protect the four faces of the combined infantry and baggage train. In more straitened circumstances, the horsemen would split into two units which formed long lines down each side of the line of march, extending ahead to defend the front and still farther behind to protect the stragglers such as any wounded.

The army continued the ancient practice of constructing fortified marching camps. Surveyors preceded the army and laid out a camp in a suitable location, marking the places for each unit by placing their standard there. As with the legions of Old Rome, such a camp was to be surrounded with a ditch and bank with L-shaped openings on each side. In addition, a strip of land was sown with caltrops in groups of nine strung on a light chain and pegged down at one end for ease of recovery. A zone providing advance warning of surreptitious nocturnal infiltration could be created by suspending bells on cords strung tightly between pegs surrounding the ditch. Within these boundaries the tents of the various units were to be pitched together laid out

G **ENCAMPED IN POTENTIALLY HOSTILE TERRITORY**

Literary sources indicate that the Roman army's time-honoured practice of building carefully organized marching camps protected by an earth rampart with L-shaped openings in potentially hostile territory was still the paradigm in the tenth and eleventh centuries. That this was not just an unrealistic wish of the manual writers is affirmed by numerous written sources in both Greek and Arabic, and on the negative side by the account of the debacle of 1049 when the general *raiktôr* Kônstantinos lost his entire force to a Patzinak surprise attack as a result of not ordering them to encamp securely. The infantry tents were placed immediately inside the perimeter, with the cavalry and their mounts nearer the centre. This was designed to minimize the chance that the enemy might contrive a means to spook the horses, therefore resulting in a destructive stampede through the camp, and to permit the infantry, who could stand to more quickly, to mount a defence against any surprise attack, thus buying time to allow the cavalry to mobilize. Once encamped, the horses were to be watered in an orderly manner rather than turned out in a mob, both for their own benefit in reducing the risk of fouling the water supply, and in the interests of security. This was to be done even in friendly territory; this was all the more imperative in less secure circumstances, where some of the cavalry always had to be held ready for action.

This warrior saint depicted in an eleventh-century fresco in the 'Hidden Church' at Göreme in Kappadokhia shows fine detail of his *klivanion* – two rivets securing the plates and two laces suspending them, and the splinted upper sleeves. The cloak and heavily trimmed brocade tunic show that this is parade dress of the courtly elite. (Photo courtesy of Steven Lowe)

in regular rows with streets in between. The substantial rope spread of the round pavilions was to be fully interlaced, partly to keep the camp somewhat compact, but also as a security measure to restrict all traffic to the designated streets where it could be better overseen, and where focused defence could be organized in the event of incursion. Where the army was a combined force, the layout of the camp was concentric with the infantry in the outer zone and cavalry around the commander at the centre. The reason for this was so that the foot soldiers would bear the brunt of any surprise attack, lessening the chance that the livestock would panic and stampede through the camp and giving the horsemen time to saddle and arm themselves for a counterattack. Where the army was composed entirely of cavalry, on the day of a battle the servants and other personnel who were normally non-combatant were left

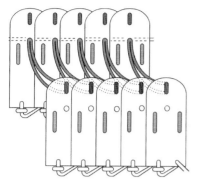 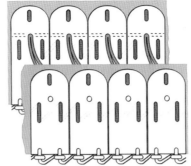 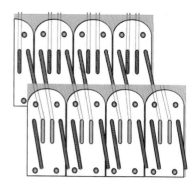

with the task of defending the camp. One unit (*vandon/allagion*) of horsemen was to be left with them, charged with the responsibility of interdicting the gates of the rampart.

Once a camp was established and the day's activities were complete, the evening meal was followed by the singing of a hymn to the Trinity, the *Trisagion*, which initiated the night's curfew. Sentries were always on duty, and were doubled during the night. Passwords were required of anyone moving about the camp and were changed on a daily basis to prevent infiltration.

Expeditionary movements were evidently episodic, with several days of marching and daily encampment broken up by a day or days in one place for recuperation, repair or training exercises. There were also inevitably periods when the weather prevented planned movement. These intervals must have been quite miserable with the men mired under wet canvas, but again they would be put to whatever good uses could be contrived. Yet there is only so much gear renovation and armour polishing that can be done and one must

ABOVE LEFT
The most long-lived and widespread construction of lamellar which was probably used throughout the period for hide horse armour, and was the starting point for Byzantine technological advances.

ABOVE CENTRE
The first stage in the evolution of Byzantine lamellar from the ubiquitous form – plates laced to a leather strip rather than to each other. For the sake of clarity a slight gap is shown between the plates, but in reality they would be as close together as possible.

ABOVE RIGHT
One of the last stages in Byzantine lamellar evolution. Double rivets and two suspensions to and from each plate make it especially resistant to damage, while the offset plates forestall direct penetration. The left margin represents the edge of the fabric, illustrating how half-plates could be used to create a straight edge.

This twelfth-century silver plate from Constantinople shows fine details. Note the scabbard under the rider's right leg. The lack of any visible fastening is not poor draughtsmanship. Arabic manuscripts show maces being carried in a similar manner, and the author's experience confirms that the rider's weight on the stirrup is quite enough to hold a weapon under the leather without any other support. (Photograph: Sam Fogg Antiquities)

A sample of middle Byzantine-era rings for archery from a major private collection. Wearing a properly fitting ring on the thumb made drawing a more powerful bow easier. (Photo courtesy of Steven Baker)

assume that the men tended to fall back on the time-honoured recreations of soldiers – drinking and gambling. Curiously, however, the one forbidden recreation that is mentioned by name in Leo's *Taktika*, for its supposed negative effects on discipline and the troops' physique, is dancing.

The campaigning season was usually confined to the period between late spring and early autumn. Outside this time the *strateioumenoi* would usually demobilize back to their farms, while the tagmatic soldiers retired to their permanent barracks. A notable exception to this rule happened in the late tenth century when Nikêforos II decided to keep his expeditionary army in the field in Kappadokhia through winter. The emperor had an entire subterranean barracks complex, comprising dormitories, refectories, storerooms and stables, cut into the rock in accordance with the ancient custom of the region. Such constructions are still commonly inhabited to this day and these cosy shelters with their raised sleeping platforms and dining benches must have been a very welcome change from the multitudinous privations of long-term life under canvas.

When the army undertook siege there was, of course, little direct involvement for the cavalry. It should not be assumed, however, that they were given a holiday. In fact they might well have had more to do, and may

Roman troops pursuing Arabs, from the illuminated *Chronicle of Skylitzes*. Although this manuscript was illustrated in Sicily in the twelfth century, it drew heavily on East Roman sources of the previous centuries as well as contemporary observation, and can sometimes show useful detail when corroborated with other sources. Note the boots with long front flaps tied up over the knee. (Biblioteca Nacionale, Madrid)

have become busier the longer the siege continued. This is because one responsibility they had to take up all the more was foraging. A besieging army would soon exhaust the supplies it had carried with it and those that could be obtained in the immediate vicinity. Thereafter the long-distance mobility of the horsemen would be essential to obtaining stocks of the provisions from farther and farther afield as the siege wore on. Period accounts record units travelling hundreds of kilometres to obtain supplies for a large army. A more familiar duty of redoubled importance during a siege was long-range scouting, lest the army be taken inadequately prepared by a relieving force. Even when the heavier troopers were engaged in such activities, and so were likely to be riding out less heavily armoured than into combat, their equipment did not necessarily lie idle. The *Syllogê Taktikôn* recommends that all such surplus gear was worn about the camp in order to give the defenders the impression of the army being more heavily equipped than it was, thereby sapping the enemy's courage and will to resist.

EXPERIENCE OF BATTLE

The battle experience of a Roman cavalryman of this era would in some respects be less variable than that of his pedestrian counterpart. The presence or absence of an infantry force would make some difference, but the main variation was between the three segments of the cavalry force. Certain practices were common across the army and served to bind its disparate elements together. The religious observances which were part of the army's daily routine were redoubled when battle was imminent. Thus, on the morning of a battle the prayer ritual was longer, and, without a doubt more

A fine example of why the illuminated *Chronicle of Skylitzes* must often be treated with considerable caution – the Romans and Arabs are completely indistinguishable. (Biblioteca Nacionale, Madrid)

heartfelt, with more of an emphasis on repentance for sin and making peace with God in the hope that a man might go into battle unconstrained by unfinished spiritual business. With this taken care of, the troops were to be provided with a solid meal before mustering to the field.

The mobility of the participants necessarily makes a cavalry battle more episodic than an infantry clash. A horseman's effectiveness reduces rapidly and his vulnerability increases a great deal as his velocity declines. Thus, the battlefield paradigm for any group of cavalry was very much like the traditional aphorism about war itself – periods of boredom interspersed with intervals of stark terror. The contrast would have been less acute when the army was operating as a purely cavalry force, for then the command and muster location was still potentially vulnerable to direct attack from enemy cavalry, and hence a much higher level of vigilance and readiness had to be maintained. Where the army had a substantial infantry component, the horsemen had the luxury of rallying, resting and re-equipping in relative security behind the front or inside the infantry square. That situation did, however, demand more discipline to counter specific risks, as forays had to be made through the limited openings in the infantry lines cleanly and without disturbing the foot soldiers or risking becoming entangled with a returning unit. This was a little easier when the infantry formed a square and therefore had more gates available, or when a linear formation could afford the luxury of open flanks, allowing the riders to flow freely around the line as well as through the gaps.

The troopers who were the first to engage and would normally have fought most consistently throughout the entire course of the battle were the archers, coursing over much greater distances to harry the enemy's advance

and then sallying again and again to barrage the opposing forces even once close combat was under way. Riding with relatively light armoured and swiftly, the main danger to them was from returning missiles, so their experience of the most immediate press of battle would have been rare and accidental. The *prokoursatôres* were closer to the cutting edge, so to speak, taking the battle to the enemy cavalry and smaller or weaker groups of infantry. They engaged with lance, sword, mace and axe, and so were much more vulnerable to severe casualties in return.

The experience of the *katafraktoi* is scarcely imaginable. Their weight, and hence relative slowness and lack of manoeuvrability, meant that they would rarely fight other cavalry. There was no nation around that could field troops as well equipped, so other horsemen would normally have avoided a head-on clash with Roman *katafraktoi*, unless they had the opportunity to mob an isolated individual or small group. The main job of the *katafraktoi* was to smash substantial infantry formations. To this end, the 'hurry up and wait' aspect of warfare would predominate, as their moment would be chosen for a hopefully decisive strike once the opposing force had been softened up somewhat by encounters with the other troops. Once they were deployed, they were formed up in a blunt wedge formation twelve ranks deep, which could be as many as 20 across the front and over 500 in total. According to Fôkas, their initial armament was mixed by rank, with the first four lines armed with maces then the rest alternating swords and spears. The unit would trot in extended order with a metre between each man until they got to within a kilometre and a half of the enemy front, then they would close up the formation until the men were virtually knee to knee. Over the remaining distance the pace was increased to a collected canter, then to an extended canter just before impact. The ideal outcome was that this human and equine juggernaut would roll over the foe and wheel about to punch back through the line from behind, and this optimal scenario must have been played out reasonably often. No contemporary nation could field troops as well trained as the Roman Empire, and none was using the long pike which is the most effective against heavy cavalry, so that the weight and impact of a wedge of *katafraktoi* would have had little trouble overwhelming a formation of infantry armed only with short spears and hand weapons, unless it had improbable depth. Not that they would expect to get through entirely unscathed. The riskiest position would probably be in the centre to middle rear of the wedge, where the danger would be more from becoming entangled with a horse and rider who had themselves fallen over the bodies of enemy soldiers.

The *defensôres* would in some ways have the most wearing part to play in a battle, holding to the discipline and patience of waiting for the moment when a returning unit was pursued by hostile cavalry and they would have to sally to drive off the pursuers. If the opposing army was light on cavalry, they might pass the entire battle with nothing to do. Even when the foe were strong in their mounted arm, they would be unlikely to launch into a full-blown engagement with the *defensôres*, and so a member of that unit might only rarely come to blows. A thoughtful *stratêgos* might in the course of a long battle replace men who had begun as *prokousatôres* with those who had entered the battle as *defensôres*, thereby spreading the exertions, and testing the mettle of all his men across their duties.

However, even when the superiority of tried and tested Roman methods were manifest there were still casualties, and it is in the arrangements for dealing with them that the army's unique strength survived. When the cavalry were operating alone, or with a linear infantry screen, an equestrian field hospital was established approximately 2,000m behind the main battle line (the infantry dressing station was nearer the front.) This was staffed by doctors for man and horse and orderlies, and was served by ambulance men called *daipotatoi* or *krivantai*. The *krivantai* were provided with their own horses so that they might ride out and recover wounded horsemen who could not make their own way back. The saddles of these mounts had an additional

---

H **EXPERIENCE OF BATTLE: DYRRAKHION, 1081**

An episode from the battle of Dyrrakhion in 1081 recounted by Anna Komnênê regarding her father, Emperor Alexios I, shows just how much protection Roman cavalry armour in the period could afford. Separated from the army, Alexios was attacked with lances from one side by three Norman knights. Since Alexios was protected by layers of padding, iron lamellar and possibly also mail, their weapons caused him no injury, but served only to partially unseat him, with the entanglement of his spurs in his horse's trapping preventing him from falling entirely. Another group of Normans charged at him in a similar way from the other side, also driving their spears at his body, yet they only succeeded in pushing him back into his saddle. At this point Alexios made his escape (Anna claims his horse bolted) with several of the Normans' lances still entangled in his *epilôrikion*. Tests conducted by the author confirm the likelihood of this account, for even when a spear point manages to slip between the plates, the outer layer tends to bind the blade, while the inner layer, commonly offset by half, like scales or roof tiles, stops the point entirely. As per the manuals, Alexios' horse is armoured with an iron headpiece, but with a chest barding made of oxhide lamellar. The construction of the horse's armour employs the original ubiquitous form of hanging lamellae as it existed before the refinements in manufacture that began to be applied to metal *klivania* for human use in the ninth century. Although both the manuals and other literary sources refer to iron headpieces for the horses of the heavy cavalry, we have neither surviving examples nor good pictures to tell us what they looked like in middle Byzantine Rômania.

This magnificent icon of Saints Sergios and Bakkhos from the turn of the thirteenth century shows exquisite realistic detail of their equipment – full scale shirts, high boots, horn-nocked recurve bows, a fine array of arrowheads corroborating those found in archaeology, and their horse furniture. Note the European-style high saddles and the so-called 'St. George cross' pennon. (Monastery of St. Catherine, Sinai)

stirrup attached to the near side rear arch to allow the *daipotatos* to mount once he had the injured trooper settled. He also carried a flask of water to help revive the wounded. The pattern of injuries probably remained pretty consistent through the length of the engagement. It would begin and continue with arrow wounds, although as horsemen were moving targets, these were probably less common than amongst the infantry. It must have had a very steadying effect for the troops to see casualties being removed systematically from the combat area and from time to time returning after treatment to bolster the units. It would be in dramatic contrast to virtually all of their enemies, amongst whom the wounded and dead merely lay where they fell, remaining in the midst of the fighting for the duration of the battle.

The first item on the agenda after a victory was the ritual of thanksgiving to God, and the burying of the dead. Some time afterwards came a parade where the events were reviewed, and soldiers who had been seen to distinguish themselves in the battle were rewarded. It appears there was some system of citation in existence, as the manuals mention both 'honours and gifts'. Amongst the physical rewards mentioned are arms and armour and shares in the booty. The officers of units that performed well were rewarded with promotion. On the other hand, men who had failed to do their duty were punished. Extreme cowardice received the universal sanction of death, while flogging, mutilation and fines were imposed for lesser failings.

Scholars have estimated that a casualty rate of 15–20 per cent was the point at which a medieval European army broke and ran. This figure must have been higher for a Roman army of this era, if only because the retrieval of the injured would somewhat disguise the issue. Of course, there were defeats. Literature of the period tends to make more of the notorious and catastrophic defeats than the 'routine' victories, yet generally these disasters were the result of failures at the command level or, as with the battle of Manzikert in 1071, a consequence of political dissension spilling over from the capital onto the battlefield. The capacity of a cavalryman to flee in the case of a reverse is, of course, much greater than that of a foot soldier, but in a combined army their discipline was all the more important, for a defeated infantry force abandoned by its cavalry is effectively doomed. The manuals go into considerable detail about steps to take in the event of a defeat, and these often hinge upon a disciplined mounted arm protecting a disordered and less capable infantry.

The javelin game known to the ancients has never fallen out of favour in Anatolia. This picture, taken in Turkey in the 1960s, shows both its enduring popularity, and the fact that the audience might be as much at risk as the players. (© National Geographic Society)

COLLECTING, MUSEUMS AND REENACTMENT

Most of the core territory of the Eastern Roman Empire in this era is now contained within the boundaries of the modern state of Turkey. Modern Turks are ambivalent, to say the least, about this portion of the Roman Empire, seeing it as 'tainted' with Hellenism, and as a result the archaeology of non-Turkish material in Anatolia is often neglected. In any case, the export of all archaeological antiquities is prohibited. Greece and the Balkans does yield a certain amount of material, but little of substance makes it onto the open market. Hence, while small and non-specific items such as buckles are often available to collectors, nothing of military significance (except, perhaps, the occasional arrowhead) is to be found on the antiquities market.

By the same token, authenticated material in museum collections is also somewhat sparse. The qualification 'authenticated' is used advisedly, as the common cultural practices of the Balkans and Caucasus and the fluid borders of the empire often make it very difficult to say with any certainty which ethnic group was likely to have originated or used any given artefact. The maritime museum at Bodrum in Turkey holds the significant assemblage from the eleventh-century Serçe Limani shipwreck, which includes some spearheads, the hilt of a sword and tools. Other weaponry is very rare, save for a considerable array of mace heads in various Bulgarian collections. Examples of the most common sort of spiked mace head have turned up from time to time in antiquities dealerships. There are just two surviving authenticated helms of the

The bronze horses looted from Constantinople and taken to Venice in 1204 represent a paradigm of the finely conformed and spirited beasts Roman horse-breeders sought to create for both the hippodrome and the battlefield. (Photograph courtesy Yann Kervran)

Koursôres in pursuit, from a late-tenth-century manuscript made in the region of Italy that remained in Roman control until the rise of the Normans in the mid-eleventh century. (Monte Cassino Monastery library)

period. The tenth-century Yasenovo helm is held in the archaeological museum at Kazanlik, Bulgaria, while a thirteenth-century parade kettle-hat inlaid with busts of saints is kept in the Hermitage Museum, St Petersburg. Weapons and pieces of lamellar found in the ruins of the Great Palace by a British excavation in the 1930s are held in the Byzantine Museum in Istanbul, but may not presently be on display.

In contrast, the physical bulwarks of the empire necessarily survive extensively. The walls of Constantinople have been subject to extensive restoration in recent years (although this has sometimes distorted the form of certain elements) and are extensively accessible over most of their length. There is a substantial and interesting later fortress at the north end of the Bosphoros readily visited by regular ferries, while Nikaia (modern Iznik) and Thessaloniki retain extensive remains of their city walls. The citadel of Ankyra (modern Ankara), built in the ninth century, is a fascinating study of the extensive re-use of antique marble, and has a distinctive form. Kappadokhia has a number of fortresses, and a subterranean barracks complex built in the tenth century. Kilikia has a wide array of quite well preserved buildings of this era with military character ranging from stronghouses to major fortresses, although generally their present form derives from Armenian work.

The hitherto low public profile of this era and area of history means that there are still relatively few avenues for re-enactment or recreation of the Roman Empire of this period, although the number is growing. Larger, broad-spectrum groups such as 'The Vikings' (UK and USA) and the 'Society for Creative Anachronism' (USA and international) embrace it as a minority interest. The 'New Varangian Guard' (Australia and elsewhere) is one well-established group with a Byzantine focus, although, as its name indicates, it leans more to the mercenary forces that converged upon the city than on native Romans. The 'Hetaireia Palatiou', or 'Palace Company', is a group in Britain that recreates aspects of the court milieu in the tenth to twelfth centuries, including ceremonial and military guard activities. In France, '1186' embraces the entire Levant in the early Crusades era, while 'La Tagma de Byzance' focuses on the Palaiologian period. 'Les Poulaines', 'I Cavalieri delle Terre Tarentine' and other groups in Italy incorporate aspects of Byzantine influence in southern Italy into their activities.

GLOSSARY

The transliteration of Greek in modern times has been traditionally contaminated by influences imported from post-Classical Latin. In this volume, the transliteration has been based upon the pronunciation of Greek as it was spoken in the period covered by this volume, which was already largely similar to modern usage. Hence beta = v and eta (ê) and omega (ô) are pronounced as 'i' and 'o' respectively. 'Kh' is a fricative or heavily accented aspirant like the 'ch' in the Scottish 'loch'. The forms given are singular. The main Greek plurals are -os>-oi, -on>-a, -a>-ai.

Allagion	The smallest unit of cavalry normally 50, but in certain cases 320, 350 or 400. Commanded by a **komês**. Otherwise called **vandon** (banner).
Daipotatos	(Latin: *deputatus*) Field medics who recovered the wounded and returned them to treatment centres. Also *despotatos*, *dipotatês* and **krivantês**.
Defensôr	A **koursôr** providing a protective screen for other troopers returning from extended operations to a camp or infantry formation. See also **prokoursatôr.**
Droungarios	Commander of a **droungos.**
Droungos	A unit of 150 or more cavalrymen. Commanded by a **droungarios.** Also *taxiarkhia.*
Doux	In the Komnenian era, a provincial governor superior in rank to a **stratêgos.**
Epilôrikion	Padded surcoat worn by cavalry, as distinct in use from **zava/kavadion**, but often similar in form.
Esôforion	Shirt or under-tunic, of usually plain, undyed linen, but sometimes striped in more fashionable use.
Gounion	Padded arming coat worn by infantry in lieu of solid armour. Parade versions were worn in imperial ceremonies by units stationed in the capital. Synonymous with **kavadion** and the earlier **zava.**
Hetaireia	Greek for 'company'. Units of the metropolitan *tagma*. Previously called *skhola.*
Hypodimata	General term for footwear, but commonly boots in this period.
Iatros	Doctor.
Kampotouva	Padded leggings.
Katafraktos	Heavy-impact cavalry. Ideally comprehensively armoured with lamellar, mail, limb pieces and *epilôrikion,* and armed with multiple weapons.

A replica of a *katafraktos* helm using the construction of the tenth-century example found at Yasenovo in Bulgaria. The horizontally segmented construction is also illustrated in the Madrid Skylitzes manuscript. The mail skirt is suspended by a method also used on other surviving Caucasian helms whereby the rings are supported by a wire running through a slotted channel in the brim. (Author's photograph)

Kavadion	Padded coat worn by infantry in lieu of solid armour. This term was also applied to civilian coats. See **gounion** and **zava**.
Klivanion	1. A corselet of **lamellar**. 2. Lamellar as a fabric of armour.
Komês	'Count'; commander of a **vandon/allagion**.
Kontarion	Spear or lance. Cavalry *kontaria* were about 2.7m long.

Koursôr	Medium cavalry. Commonly armoured in mail or scale. Such men performed the roles of **prokoursatôr** or **defensôr**. This is the origin of the later European term and troop type 'Hussar'.
Krivantês	Field medics who recovered the wounded and returned them to treatment centres. Also **daipotatos**, *despotatos* and *dipotatês*.
Lamellar	Armour made of plates of metal, horn or leather fastened together with cordage, or, in the Eastern Roman Empire uniquely, a mixture of rivets and cordage, in which the rows of plates overlap upwards in normal use. Sometimes used on limb pieces inverted, thus overlapping downwards but still with the same construction, as distinct from **scale armour.**
Lôrikion	Usually a mail shirt. *Alusidôton*: literally 'chain armour'. *Folidôton*: a garment of scales.
Mandatôr	Functionary who carried orders from the high command to front-line officers.
Matzouka	An impact weapon with a metal head on a wooden shaft – mace. See **spathovaklion** and **sideroravdion**.
Meros	See **tourma.**
Minsouratôr	A surveyor sent ahead of the army on campaign to lay out the campsite. Also *minsôr*.
Paramêrion	A single-edged slightly curved sword hung horizontally from a shoulder strap or belt and used by all types of troops.
Paximata	Also *paximadion*. Hardtack made of course-ground wholemeal flour double baked, and possibly also containing other dried foods such as fruit and meat.
Pektorarion	A coloured cloth band tied around the chest to signal rank.
Prokoursatôr	A **koursôr** engaged in extended operations, such as scouting or pursuing and harassing smaller or detached groups of enemy.
Roukhon	Main body garment – tunic.
Sideroravdion	A shafted impact weapon (mace) made entirely of iron. Probably synonymous with **spathovaklion**.
Spathion	(Latin: *spatha*) A double-edged straight sword used by all types of troops. The standard form was hung vertically from a shoulder strap like the ancient *gladius*. Another type used for lighter armoured troops and for parade purposes was hung horizontally from a belt: *zôstikion*.

Spathovaklion	A shafted impact weapon (mace) made entirely of iron with a guard and hilt like a sword. Probably synonymous with **sideroravdion.**
Strateia	The obligation to provide a soldier, other military services or money in exchange for tenure of land. See **strateioumenos.**
Strateioumenos	A man discharging the service obligations of **strateia.**
Stratos	The army overall.
Tagma	A unit of the army, or the army in general. Plural: *tagmata.*
Taxiarkhia	See **droungos.**
Taxiarkhês	Commander of a **taxiarkhia.**
Therapeutês	A (male) nurse or orderly in a field hospital or dressing station.
Tourma	A unit of 1,350 or more horsemen. Commanded by a **Tourmarkhês.**
Tourmarkhês	Commander of a **tourma.**
Tzangia	Calf-length boots.
Tzervoulia	Sturdy, rustic shoes.
Tzikourion	A battleaxe, commonly with one standard blade and a hammer, spike or knife-like blade.
Skoutarion	General term for a shield.
Stratêgos	'General'. Commonly a *stratêgos* served as a provincial governor in the earlier part of the period (see **thêma, doux**), but might serve in a purely military capacity.
Thêma	A province. By the middle Byzantine period thematic organization was somewhat tenuous, but a thematic **stratêgos** or **doux** was still expected to raise troops for a campaign in his region.
Vandon	'Banner'. In addition to a flag, this term also refers to a unit. See **allagion.**
Voukinatôr	(Latin: *bucinator*) Trumpeter.
Zava	In earlier usage, flexible body armour, which might be a padded arming coat worn in lieu of solid armour, or a shirt of mail or scales. By the tenth century it had been supplanted by consistent use of more specific terms – **kavadion, lôrikion** etc – and had come to mean mail pieces used to supplement more solid armour, usually for cavalry.

INDEX

References to illustrations are shown in **bold**.

GOING FOR A SONG

GOING FOR A SONG

An anthology of poems about antiques

Compiled and introduced by
BEVIS HILLIER

with 94 Illustrations by Peter MacKarell

HOPCYN PRESS

First published in Britain in 2014 by Hopcyn Press Limited.

The right by Bevis Hillier to be identified as the Author of the Work has been asserted by him in accordance with the Copyright, Designs and Patents Act 1988.

ISBN: 978-0-9572977-3-9

Manuscript typed by Secret Genius, Winchester, SO23 8GH
www.secretgenius.co.uk

Printed and bound by Imago Ltd

DEAR OLD FRIEND
PETER THIS BOOK
IS DEDICATED TO
YOUR MEMORY
AND TO JOAN
CHRISTY AND
JOHANNA RIP

Contents

Introduction

Poets have something in common with collectors. Both assemble images, whether physical or literal, and arrange them in sequences: the collector on shelves, the poet in lines. Both the choice and the arrangement of images are at the despotic discretion of poet or collector – a power limited only by mind or purse, respectively.

In this book, the two kinds of collection are allied – rather as two antique collections were brought together by the marriage of their owners in the last novel L.P. Hartley wrote, *The Collectors*. (A more metaphorical link between antiques and poetry was found in the title of the long-running television series that starred Arthur Negus – *Going for a Song*.)

The present book is an anthology of poems about antiques: either poems about objects which had already become antique at the time of writing (for example, the Victorian Austin Dobson on Madame de Pompadour's fan) or poems about objects which were not antique at the time of writing, but have since become antiques (the contents of Swift's room, or Cowper's reading-chair). It ranges from great poems such as Keats's 'Ode to a Grecian Urn' to comic verse such as that by the late Alistair Sampson, an antique dealer in Knightsbridge, London. In 1984, when I left for California for five years, Sampson succeeded me as Collecting columnist of Alan Coren's *Punch*. His *Times* obituary was almost entirely devoted to that aspect of his career, but I think he was far more significant as a truly comedic poet.

The anthology was conceived as a light-hearted exercise, and the illustrations by the late Peter MacKarell were drawn in the same spirit. The occasional anachronisms in the drawings are of course deliberate: I must plead heinously guilty to having suggested the Mona Lisa in a snorkel and flippers to illustrate the line 'She has been a diver in deep seas' from Yeats's poetic adaptation of Pater's lines about La Gioconda. Giving the book a title was a problem. *Over is Their Antique Joy*, from Yeats's 'The woods of Arcady are dead' seemed a little portentous. The mildly punning title finally chosen won a narrow victory over *The Poetry of Antiques*.

The poems selected span just over nine centuries, but certain themes recur again and again. The most popular is the idea of the antique as a fetish-object which has soaked up some of the history to which it was witness – a talisman that can help us to conjure the past. In its least sophisticated form, this idea is responsible for many poems of the 'What changes you must have seen!' kind. My favourite among these is Horace Smith's 'Address to the Mummy in Belzoni's Exhibition' (1819):

> Did'st thou not hear the pother o'er thy head,
> When the great Persian conqueror, Cambyses,
> Marched armies o'er thy tomb with thundering tread,
> O'erthrew Osiris, Orus, Apis, Isis?
> And shook the pyramids with fear and wonder,
> When the gigantic Memnon fell asunder?

The idea inspires more profound thoughts in contemporary poets. Anthony Thwaite (who is a collector, and has written learnedly on Bellarmine jugs in *The Connoisseur* magazine) writes of a 'blue-dash charger' depicting Adam and Eve:

> A pure ornament,
> An object for one who collects
> Objects, it covers a span
> More than its surface, a truth...

While William Empson, in his 'Homage to the British Museum', writes of a primitive toad-shaped god in the Ethnological Section (now the Museum of Mankind):

> His smooth wood creeps with all the creeds of the world.
> Attending there let us absorb the cultures of nations
> And dissolve into our judgment all their codes...

Here again is the idea that a particular antique has absorbed something of an earlier time and a different culture, something we may be able to distil or decipher from it.

In several other poems, antiques are made catalysts for purely personal memories: Thackeray's cane-bottomed chair, Eliza Cook's old armchair and old clock, the treasure-box of Robert Graves's 'Ann in chill moonlight', or the brass button of Sir Osbert Sitwell's old sahib:

> He carried in his pocket together
> This button and a desiccated potato;
> They both possessed a power
> But the potato proved less potent,
> Could only ward off pain:
> Whereas the button at a touch
> Fastened two worlds together distant in time and space.

While some of the poets think antiques help one to recover the past, others see them as poignant relics of a past which can never be restored, reminding us of past ideals superior to those of the present. Robert Bridges says of the crusader on a church brass:

> Would we could teach our sons
> His trust in face of doom.

L.P. Hartley wrote, in *The Collectors*: 'It seems to me, in these rather sad days, that some people attach more importance, and more affection, to the relics of the past, than they do to their fellow human beings – an object from long ago embodies something we can't recover, because it springs from an impulse which we have outlived, and can only substitute for it images derived from the workings of the mind – laboratory experiments, in fact.'

The frailty of antiques is another recurring theme, sometimes as an emblem of human impermanence, sometimes to mock the vanity of setting store by such perishable works, sometimes for sheer comic effect. Laurence Whyte, a Dublin poet writing in 1742, comments in 'The Broken Mug':

Thou best of MUGS for e'er adieu
Since I am doomed to follow you:
I am but *Clay*, and so wert *Thou*...

John Gay equates the delicacy of old porcelain to the frailty whose name is woman:

Vessels so pure, and so refined,
Appear the types of woman-kind:
Are they not valued for their beauty,
Too fair, too fine, for household duty?...
I grant they're frail yet they're so rare,
The treasure cannot cost too dear!

Two of Byron's contributions to this book are on the romantic notion of the ephemeral nature of human pleasures – an idea especially piquant when one is still enjoying them. His cup formed from a human skull is

the only skull,
From which, unlike a living head,
Whatever flows is never dull.

Such a cup, made for one of the Bonaparte-Wyse family, was sold at Christie's in 1968, when I was sale room correspondent of *The Times*.

The greatest poem using an antique as illustration of *Sic transit gloria mundi* is Shelley's 'Ozymandias', written ten years after Byron's skull poem. The later requiems for antiques in this book are all comic, whether by intention or not: Coleridge's 'Monody on a Tea Kettle', George Thornbury's 'Melting the Earl's Plate', Ella Wheeler Wilcox's 'An Old Fan'. Tom Hood's 'The China Mender' is a slapstick classic on breakage, enjoyable as a crockery-shy at a fair:

I'm very much mistook if Mr Lambert's will be a catch;
The breaking of the Chiny will be the breaking off of his own match.
Missis wouldn't have an angel, if he was careless about Chiny;
She never forgives a chip, if it's ever so small and tiny.
Lawk! I never saw a man in all my life in such a taking;
I could find in my heart to pity him for all his mischief-making.
To see him stand a-hammering and stammering, like a zany;
But what signifies apologies, if they won't mend old Chaney?
If he sent her up whole crates full, from Wedgwood's and Mr Spode's,
He couldn't make amends from the crack'd mandarins and smash'd toads...

Many of the poems are satires on the collector. There is the man who collects for collecting's sake, or because it is the fashion, and has no understanding of the antiques he has bought. One of the earliest poems in the book, published Wynkyn de Worde in 1508, puts these lines into the mouth of the book-collector on board the ship of fools:

Still I am busy bookes assembling,
For to have plenty it is a pleasant thing
In my conceyt, and to have them aye in hande:
But what they mean do I not understande...

Two centuries later, Pope is making exactly the same joke about the Earl of Burlington:

His study! with what authors is it stored?
In books, not authors, curious is my lord;
To all their dated backs he turns you round;
These Aldus printed, those Du Sueil has bound.
Lo, some are vellum, and the rest as good,
For all his lordship knows, but they are wood.

Bramston gives a similar impression of a picture-collector in 'The Man of Taste':

In curious paintings I'm exceeding nice,
And know their several beauties by their price.
Auctions and sales I constantly attend,
But chuse my pictures by a skilful friend.
Originals and copies much the same,
The picture's value is the painter's name.

The undiscriminating collector, with his hoard of miscellaneous junk, is also ridiculed. This is the one who collects in the same way as the ninth-century Welshman Nennius wrote history. '*Coacervavi*,' said Nennius, '*omne quod inveni*' – 'I have made a heap of all that I have found.' A good example of the Nennian method of collecting is given by Burns in 'Captain Grose's Peregrinations through the Highlands':

He had a rowth o' auld nick-nackets,
Rusty airn cups and jinglin'-jackets
Would hold the Loudons three in tackets
    A towmond gude;
And parritch-pots and auld saut-buckets,
    Afore the flude.

George Colman's Ozias Polyglot (poem 29) is another Nennian:

In every bedroom there were placed
Knick-knackeries of wondrous taste,
With shells and spars, stuffed birds, and flies in amber;
And by the side of every bed
There stood a Grecian urn instead
Of what is called in France a *pot-de-chambre*.

But if the poets are harsh on the collector who puts the collection above the things collected, they are merciless to him whose love for his collection exceeds, or is a substitute for, his love for his fellow humans. (The best-known example was Sir William Hamilton, the *mari complaisant* of Lord Nelson's lover – Hamilton had the misfortune to lose many of his Greek vases in a shipwreck.) Austin Dobson's 'Virtuoso', who is proud of his Dürer figure 'Charity', refuses to give a penny for war victims. Gay's lady is besotted with old china to the despair of her suitors:

> What ecstasies her bosom fire!
> How her eyes languish with desire!
> How blest, how happy should I be,
> Were that fond glance bestow'd on me!
> New doubts and fears within me war:
> What rival's near? A china jar.

Garrick, in his verse prologue to Samuel Foote's play *Taste* (1753) imputed positive frigidity to collectors:

> Why laugh at TASTE? It is a harmless Fashion,
> And quite subdues each detrimental Passion;
> The Fair ones' Hearts will ne'er incline to Man
> While they thus rage for – China and Japan.
> The Virtuoso, too, and Connoisseur,
> As ever decent, delicate and pure;
> The smallest Hair their looser Thoughts might hold,
> Just warm when Single, and when Married cold:
> Their Blood at Sight of Beauty gently flows;
> Their Venus must be old, and want a Nose!

One is reminded of a poem not in this anthology – Yeats's 'The Scholars', in which bald-headed dryasdusts

> Edit and annotate the lines
> That young men, tossing on their beds,
> Rhymed out in love's despair
> To flatter beauty's ignorant ear.

What would the scholars say, Yeats asks, 'should their Catullus walk that way?' Antique collecting can seem a form of platonic necrophilia, a perverse preference for the dead instead of the quick. Walter de la Mare amusingly presents the two in juxtaposition in a local museum:

> They stood – rain pelting at window, shrouded sea –
> Tenderly hand in hand, too happy to talk;
> And there, its amorous eye intent on me,
> *Plautus impennis*, the extinct Great Auk.

If the man who collects is not devoid of feelings, then he is at least considered effeminate, as the dying captain of Kipling's *Mary Gloster* plainly suggests in his deathbed homily to his 'Harrer and Trinity College' educated son:

> The things I knew was proper you wouldn't thank me to give,
> And the things I knew was rotten you said was the way to live.
> For you muddled with books and pictures, an' china an' etchin's an' fans,
> And your rooms at college was beastly – more like a whore's than a man's.

That sort of attitude was already evident in the eighteenth century. Admiral Byng collected china. When he was court-martialled for alleged cowardice (he was executed), caricaturists showed him in his cabin, with porcelain on all the shelves to suggest a lack of virility.

The collector as dupe is made to seem as unengaging as the collector as cunning, avaricious exploiter. To Pope, Sir Andrew Fountaine was 'False as his gems and cancer'd as his coins'. The Irish peasants of John Stevenson's 'The Antiquary' snigger at the old stones and rusty buckles that the visiting scholar is so eager to find. A.D. Godley (better known as the author of 'The Motor Bus' – 'What is it that roareth thus?') gets his own back on antique creation by mocking as 'paltry rubbish' a graven image that seems to be giving itself airs and graces. Sir William Hamilton is jocularly accused of faking his Etruscan antiques and baking them himself. Alistair Sampson's collector pays ten shillings for a vase at a church bazaar:

> 'Ten bob,' she said, and blew a kiss.
> 'The Vicar will be told of this.'
> 'Will he?' I said, and left the grounds.
> The vase is worth ten thousand pounds.

Naturally dealers and auctioneers get their share of odium. Every collector will be familiar with the kind of dealer portrayed in Sampson's poem 'Fenders' – who swears blind that a particular kind of antique is rare and costly until you reveal that you want to sell one, not buy, when the tune changes. And every dealer will recognize the genteel lady of Sampson's 'A Dealer Visits', who will ask every question about the antique she owns except the one she really wants answered: '*How much is it worth?*' Sampson's most fiendish creation was the uncle who collected glass eyes:

> He never used the things himself –
> He kept them glaring on a shelf.
> And champing on the shelf beneath
> Were twenty-seven sets of teeth.

The degradation of cherished possessions when they are put to auction is the subject of more than one of the poems. The earliest treatment of the subject is by Otway:

> I passed this very moment by thy doors,
> And found them guarded by a troop of villains;
> The sons of public rapine were destroying.
> They told me, by the sentence of the law,
> They had commission to seize all thy fortune.

Here stood a ruffian with a horrid face,
Lording it o'er a heap of massive plate,
Tumbled into a heap for public sale;
There was another making villainous jests
At thy undoing; he had ta'en possession
Of all thy ancient, most domestic ornaments,
Rich hangings intermixed, and wrought with gold.
Thy very bed was violated
By the coarse hands of filthy dungeon slaves,
And thrown amidst the common lumber!

Those lines could have served as a description of the sale-of-contents of Oscar Wilde's Tite Street house after his trial in 1895 – a scene evoked in all its cruelty by William Gaunt in *The Æsthetic Adventure*:

The artist, who had been rash enough to try conclusions
with society was sold up. An inquisitive, careless rabble
tramped through the rooms, and there was scarcely an
appearance of order about the sale. Yet again, a collection
of 'blue and white' was dispersed. Whistlers went for
a pound or two. Letters and manuscripts disappeared
without trace. In this way the Philistines took a
disgraceful advantage of their enemy's fall. Like the
medieval townsfolk of Pater's story they would have
plucked this Dionysus of the vine and the reed limb from
limb, if they had been able.

Wilde had himself written a poem on the sale of Keats's love-letters, melodramatically comparing that act with dice-throwing for Christ's garments. The same kind of idea is expressed in C. Day Lewis's poem 'Lot 96' about an iron fender which in the saleroom reflects 'not a ghost of the lives that illumed it':

This lot was part of their precious bond, almost
A property of its meaning. Here, in the litter
Washed up by death, values are re-assessed
At a nod from the highest bidder.

When some letters of A.E. Housman were sold at Sotheby's in 1968, I began my article on the sale in *The Times* with a verse parody of Housman, commenting on this obliviousness of the auction-room, and I have taken the liberty of including it in the anthology – rather as Alfred Hitchcock gave himself a 'cameo' appearance in his films.

On disregard of beauty, a natural subject for poets, Samuel Butler's 'Psalm of Montreal', containing the immortal catch-phrase 'O God! O Montreal!' is not to be bettered. At the opposite pole – reverence for egregious junk – C.S. Calverley has surely preserved the goofiest collector of all time, the man who saved in a glass case some cherry-stones spat out by the Prince of Wales:

My Cherrystones! I prize them,
No tongue can tell how much!
Each lady caller eyes them,
And madly longs to touch!

(Was he actually the soppiest collector? In America, some people collect strands of barbed wire. They have their own magazine, *Barbed Comments*. And I once met a man who collected aeroplane sick-bags – one was decorated with a spray of flowers and the legend 'For motion discomfort'.)

But while the poets may send up the weirder collectors, they are sympathetic to the 'mystique' of collecting on its higher levels. Andrew Lang wrote:

There's a joy without canker or cark,
There's a pleasure eternally new,
'Tis to gaze on the glaze and the mark
Of china that's ancient and blue;
Unchipp'd all the centuries through,
It has pass'd, since the chime of it rang,
And they fashion'd it, figure and hue,
In the reign of the Emperor Hwang.

Implicit in those lines is the kind of thing people say about their dogs and other pets: *they* never let you down, like human beings. That idea almost becomes explicit in the *envoi* to Lang's 'Ballade of the Book-Hunter':

Prince, all the things that tease and please –
Fame, hope, wealth, kisses, cheers and tears –
What are they but such toys as these –
Aldines, Bodonis, Elzevirs?

I originally intended to place the poems in the chronological order of the antiquities and antiques described; but I have decided instead to put them in an order (or disorder) which will give the reader more variety, interleaving older and newer, longer and shorter, the moving and the funny. However, at the eleventh hour of editing the book, I learned that my old friend John Mallet – formerly head of the Ceramics Department at the Victoria & Albert Museum – had written poems about art and antiques. They struck me as combining intellect and emotion (and some humour), and John was persuaded to let them appear *en bloc*, near the end of the book. My apologies to any living poet who feels that his or her golden lines have been shamefully omitted.

There are more poems in the book by Austin Dobson (1840–1921) than by any other poet. Dobson was a collector and made himself *the* authority of his day on eighteenth-century life and literature. It needs only the alteration of one consonant in his surname to change it into that of Ernest Dowson (1867–1900). Dowson is a greater poet than Dobson – T.S. Eliot thought him the best of all his contemporaries. He had the true poetic *ichor*. Phrases and lines of his have embedded themselves in cultural memory in a way that none of Dobson's has – 'I have been faithful to thee, Cynara! in my fashion'; 'And I was desolate and sick of an old passion'; 'days of wine and roses'. But he is for ever branded as a 'decadent', a *Yellow Book* man. His parents both commit suicide, his mother by hanging; he falls desperately in love with Missie, a twelve-year-old waitress in a Soho restaurant; his poems and letters are full of paedophilia; he dies of consumption.

Dobson, by contrast, is an ultra-respectable Victorian *paterfamilias*, father of five sons and five daughters. He joins the Board of Trade in 1856 and serves there, in high-class drudgework, until his retirement in 1901. Edmund Gosse, after a spell in the British Museum reading-room, joined him there; and one of Max Beerbohm's most comic cartoons shows the two men busy composing a ballade when suddenly, there enters the room their dour boss, Joseph Chamberlain, president of the Board of Trade.

SCENE: THE BOARD OF TRADE. TIME: OFFICE HOURS IX. THE EARLY EIGHTIES MR. AUSTIN DOBSON AND MR. EDMUND GOSSE, COMPSOING A BALLADE, ARE TAKEN UNAWARES BY THEIR PRESIDENT, MR. JOS. CHAMBERLAIN.

Dobson never rises to the heights, nor sinks to the depths, of Dowson, though S.L. Gwynn could write of him, in the *Dictionary of National Biography*:

> Nobody could read the best of his verse – and at least fifty pieces were of his best – without delight in the witty invention, the ease of movement and the exquisite finish in the style of Restoration poetry that had his verses likened to 'Dresden china'.

But what Dobson could do, and Dowson could not, was to enter – virtually to inhabit – other periods of history, capturing the Zeitgeist.

I have the same kind of feeling about the late Peter MacKarell, who illustrated most of the poems in this book. If it had been possible for Aubrey Beardsley to illustrate it, his drawings would have been finer than Peter's, and the originals would sell for thousands at auction. But like Dowson (a friend of his), Beardsley is immitigably 'decadent'. He never escapes the coils of Art Nouveau. Again, like Dowson, he dies of tuberculosis – Oscar Wilde commented, with callous wit, 'Even his lungs are affected.' MacKarell, like Dobson, can infiltrate any historical period, any country or civilization, and effortlessly evoke it. He almost always gets the period detail just right; though I note that with Browning's 'My Last Duchess' (poem 61), he makes a slight slip-up, omitting the curtain in front of the Renaissance portrait that the widowed Duke draws aside, in the poem, to reveal it to select visitors.

Peter and his wife Joan (he portrays both of them, to the life, in Fig. 75) were among my best friends in the 1970s. He taught art at Goldsmiths' College and illustrated books for the Whittington Press – now themselves collectors' items – including my *Punorama* (1972) and John St John's *To the War with Waugh* (1974). In reviewing the latter book, the old soldier Bernard Fergusson (Lord Ballantrae) gave special praise to Peter's drawings. They were half-way between cartoons and works of art: the ideal style for the present book. Multiple sclerosis robbed Peter, first of his sight and then of his life.

He illustrated almost all the poems I had chosen, but illness overtook him before he could quite complete the work – so a few are printed with no accompaniment. I am particularly sorry that he was not able to pit his talent against the writhings of the Laocoön.

The book is dedicated to Peter's memory, and to Joan and their children, Christy and Johanna.

1

A Medieval Bibliomane

I am the first fool of the whole navie
To keep the poupe, the helme, and eke the sayle:
For this is my minde, this one pleasure have I,
Of bookes to have greate plentie and apparayle.
Still I am busy bookes assembling,
For to have plenty it is a pleasant thing
In my conceyt, and to have them aye to handle:
But what they meane do I not understande.
But yet I have them in great reverence
And honoure, saving them from filth and ordure,
By often brushing and much diligence;
Full goodly bound in pleasaunt coverture,
Of damas, satten, or else of velvet pure:
I keepe them sure, fearing least they should be lost,
For in them is the cunning wherein I me boast.

Alexander Barclay
(translated from Brandt's *Ship of Fools*)

These lines, first printed
by Wynkyn de Worde in
1508, are the first known
satire on an English
collector.

2

Upon his Drinking a Bowl

Vulcan, contrive me such a cup
As Nestor used of old.
Show all thy skill to trim it up;
Damask it round with gold.

Make it so large that, filled with sack
Up to the swelling brim,
Vast toasts on the delicious lake
Like ships at sea may swim.

Engrave me battle on his cheek:
With war I've nought to do;
I'm none of those that took Maastricht,
Nor Yarmouth leaguer knew.

Let it no name of planets tell,
Fixed stars, or constellations;
For I am no Sir Sidrophel,
Nor none of my relations.

But carve thereon a spreading vine,
Then add two lovely boys;
Their limbs in amorous folds entwine,
The type of future joys.

John Wilmot, Earl of Rochester (1647–80)

The poem is a translation of Ronsard's lines beginning 'Vulcan! En faveur de moy...' As described in the *Iliad*, Nestor's 'beautifully wrought cup ... was set with golden nails, the eared handles upon it were four, and on either side there were fashioned two doves of gold, feeding, and there were double bases beneath it. Another man with great effort could lift it full from the table, but Nestor, aged as he was, lifted it without strain.' (Trans. Richmond Lattimore, xi, 631–6).

I have omitted the last stanza of Rochester's poem. To have included it would have severely limited the possible circulation of this book.

3

The Man of Taste

In curious paintings I'm exceeding nice,
And know their several beauties by their price.
Auctions and sales I constantly attend,
But chuse my pictures by a skilful friend.
Originals and copies much the same,
The picture's value is the painter's name.

My taste in sculpture from my choice is seen,
I buy no statues that are not obscene.
In spite of Addison and ancient Rome,
Sir Cloudesly Shovel's is my fav'rite tomb.
How oft have I with admiration stood,
To view with some city-magistrate in wood!
I gaze with pleasure on a lord may'r's head,
Cast with propriety in gilded lead.
Oh could I view, through London as I pass,
Some broad Sir Balaam in Corinthian brass!
High on a pedestal, ye freemen, place
His magisterial paunch and griping face;
Letter'd and gilt, let him adorn Cheapside,
And grant the tradesman what a king's deny'd.

Old coins and medals I collect, 'tis true,
Sir Andrew has 'em, and I'll have 'em too.
But among friends, if I the truth might speak,
I like the modern, and despise th'antique.
Tho' in the drawers of my japan bureau
To Lady Gripewell I the Caesars shew,
'Tis equal to her ladyship or me,
A Copper Otho, or a Scotch baubee.

J. Bramston
(British Library Ref. 12315.f.17)

The 'Sir Andrew' mentioned in the last eight lines of the poem is Sir Andrew Fountaine – see Pope's lines on him, No. 88.

SIR BALAAM
MOUNTEBANK

4

The Old Clock

Clock of the household! few creatures would trace
Aught worthy a song in thy dust-covered face;
The sight of thy hands and the sound of thy bell
Tell the hour, and to many 'tis *all* thou canst tell.
But to me thou canst preach with the tongue of a sage,
Thou canst tell me old tales from life's earliest page;
The long night of sorrow, the short span of glee –
All my chequers of fate have been witnessed by thee.

They say my first breathings of infant delight
Were bestowed on the 'dicky birds,' gilded and bright,
Which shone forth on thy case, – that the cake or the toy
Ne'er illumined my eyes with such beamings of joy.
Full well I remember my wonder profound –
What caused thee to tick and thy hands to move round,
Till I watched a safe moment and mounted the chair,
Intent to discover the why and the where.

I revelled in ruin 'mid wheels, weights, and springs;
What sport for the fingers, what glorious things!
No doubt I gained something of knowledge, but lo!
Full soon 'twas declared 'the old clock didn't go.'
The culprit was seized, but, all punishment vain;
I was caught at such doings again and again.
'Twas the favourite mischief, and nothing would cure,
Till a lock kept the pendulum sacred and sure.

The corner thou stood'st in was always my place,
When 'I shall' or 'I shan't' had insured my disgrace;
Where my storm of defiance might wear itself out,
Till the happy laugh banished the frown and the pout.
When a playmate was coming, how often my eye
Would greet thee to see if the moment were nigh;
And impatiently fancied I never had found
Thy hand such a laggard in travelling round.

Thou bringest back visions of heart-bounding times,
When thy midnight hour chorused the rude carol rhymes;
When our Christmas was noted for festival mirth,
And the merry New Year had a boisterous birth.
I remember the station thou hadst in the hall,
Where the holly and mistletoe decked the rough wall;
Where we mocked at thy voice till the herald of day
Peeped over the hills in his mantle of grey.

And thou bringest back sorrow, for oh! thou hast been
The companion of many a gloomier scene:
In the dead of the night I have heard thy loud tick,
Till my ear has recoiled and my heart has turned sick,
I have signed back to thee as I noiselessly crept
To the close-curtained bed where a dying one slept;
When thy echoing stroke and a mother's faint breath
Seemed the sepulchre tidings that whispered of death.

George Colman the Younger (1762–1836)

5

On a Lady on Her Passion for Old China

What ecstasies her bosom fire!
How her eyes languish with desire!
How blest, how happy should I be,
Were that fond glance bestow'd on me!
New doubts and fears within me war:
What rival's near? a china jar.

China's the passion of her soul;
A cup, a plate, a dish, a bowl,
Can kindle wishes in her breast,
Inflame with joy, or break her rest.

Some gems collect; some medals prize,
And view the rust with lover's eyes;
Some court the stars at midnight hours;
Some dote on Nature's charms in flowers!
But ev'ry beauty I can trace
In Laura's mind, in Laura's face;
My stars are in this brighter sphere,
My lily and my rose are here.

Philosophers more grave than wise
Hunt science down in butterflies;
Or fondly poring on a spider
Stretch human contemplation wider;
Fossils give joy to Galen's soul,
He digs for knowledge like a mole;
In shells so learn'd, that all agree
No fish that swims knows more than he!
In such pursuits if wisdom lies,
Who, Laura, shall thy taste despise?

When I some antique jar behold,
Or white, or blue, or speck'd with gold,
Vessels so pure, and so refined,
Appear the types of woman-kind:
Are they not valued for their beauty,
Too fair, too fine, for household duty?
With flowers and gold and azure dyed,

Of ev'ry house the grace and pride?
How white, how polish'd is their skin,
And valued most when only seen!
She who before was highest prized,
Is for a crack or flaw despised;
I grant they're frail yet they're so rare,
The treasure cannot cost too dear!
But man is made of coarser stuff,
And serves convenience well enough;
He's a strong earthen vessel made,
For drudging, labour, toil and trade;
And when wives lose their other self,
With ease they bear the loss of delf.

Husbands more covetous than sage
Condemn this china-buying rage;
They count that woman's prudence little,
Who sets her heart on things so brittle.
But are those wise men's inclinations
Fixt on more strong, more sure foundations?
If all that's frail we must despise,
No human view or scheme is wise.
Are not ambition's hopes as weak?
They swell like bubbles, shine and break.
A courtier's promise is so slight,
'Tis made at noon, and broke at night.
What pleasure's sure? The miss you keep
Breaks both your fortune and your sleep.
The man who loves a country life
Breaks all the comforts of his wife;
And if he quit his farm and plough,
His wife in town may break her vow.
Love, Laura, love while youth is warm,
For each new winter breaks a charm,
And woman's not like china sold,
But cheaper grows in growing old;
Then quickly choose the prudent part,
Or else you break a faithful heart.

John Gay (1685–1732)

6

The Old Sedan Chair

'What's not destroy'd by Time's devouring Hand?
Where's Troy, and where's the May-Pole in the Strand?

Bramston's 'Art of Politicks'

It stands in the stable-yard under the eaves,
Propped up by a broom-stick and covered with leaves;
It once was the pride of the gay and the fair,
But now 'tis a ruin, – that old Sedan chair!

It is battered and tattered, – it little avails
That once it was lacquered, and glistened with nails;
For its leather is cracked into lozenge and square,
Like a canvas by Wilkie, – that old Sedan chair!

See, – here come the bearing-straps; here were the holes
For the poles of the bearers – when once there were poles;
It was cushioned with silk, it was wadded with hair.
As the birds have discovered, – that old Sedan chair!

'Where's Troy?' says the poet! Look, – under the seat,
Is a nest with four eggs, – 'tis the favoured retreat
Of the Muscovy hen, who has hatched, I dare swear,
Quite an army of chicks in that old Sedan chair!

And yet – Can't you fancy a face in the frame
Of the window, – some high-headed damsel or dame,
Be-patched and be-powdered, just set by the stair,
While they raise up the lid of that old Sedan chair!

Can't you fancy Sir Plume, as beside her he stands,
With his ruffles a-droop on his delicate hands,
With his cinnamon coat, with his laced solitaire,
As he lifts her out light from that old Sedan chair?

Then it swings away slowly. Ah, many a league
It has trotted 'twixt sturdy-legged Terence and Teague;
Stout fellows! – but prone, on a question of fare,
To brandish the poles of that old Sedan chair!
It has waited by portals where Garrick has played:
It has waited by Heidegger's 'Grand Masquerade';
For my Lady Codille, for my Lady Bellair,
It has waited – and waited, that old Sedan chair!

Oh; the scandals it knows! Oh, the tales it could tell
Of Drum and Ridotto, of Rake and of Belle, –
Of cock-fight and Levée, and (scarcely more rare!)
Of Fête-days at Tyburn, that old Sedan chair.

'Heu! Quantum mutata,' I say as I go.
It deserves better fate than a stable-yard, though!
We must furbish it up, and dispatch it, –'With Care.' –
To a Fine-Art Museum – that old Sedan chair!

Austin Dobson (1840–1921)

7

A Brass Button

When for a moment braving the dust
I open a black leather box cherished in childhood
To find, among the coins,
A brass button bearing upon it a dragon,
The crest of a long-disbanded regiment,
From this black coffin there emerges,
Not the image of some Rotarian-faced Roman Emperor,
Nor of a playing-card king of the Gothic time,
But the figure of Major Postlethwaite.
Then the very clinking of the coins I touch
Becomes the rattle and obsolete jingle of spurs,
Until at last aware that a friend craves remembrance,
I sit back in my chair, allow
This lovable military ghost to assume command,
To blossom and expand and take on substance.

In his pocket he carried this button,
Which he gave me towards the end of his life,
Because, he said, he knew that I 'collected things',
But in reality because he wanted it deposited
With someone younger, very much younger,
Wanted to know it laid up safely,
Respected, venerated as he venerated it,
Before he left it, parted from it for ever.

He carried in his pocket together
This button and a desiccated potato;
They both possessed a power
But the potato proved less potent,
Could only ward off pain:
Whereas the button at a touch
Fastened two worlds together distant in time and space.

A world of old and tamed gorillas
Carrying prayer-books, decked in a joyless, respectable riot

Of plush and velvet and fur and feather and silk –
This ordered world of asphalt and stone border,
Where every stunted tree is a sign-board to the wind's direction
(The winter wind that ever seeps inland
Toward the Cemetery,
Full of bones and everlasting-flowers),
It joined, this powerful button, to a world
Where he could feel again
The parrot-feathered, tropic breeze;
Where he could see again
The sepoys, spices, emeralds and the serpents,
The turbaned princes and hell-painted priests,
The fakirs crouching high up on their pillars,
The nails of their fingers piercing their mortified flesh,
The peacock flaunting its fan across white marble,
The elephants with trunks uplifted
Trumpeting gigantic salutations,
The fluttering, shrilling parakeet

Mocking the jewelled mutterings of the Indian heat.
Was it for this,
To be an unseen shadow, strealing
Among those other cheap diurnal shadows,
Was it for this,
That Major Postlethwaite had fired his powder
Against th'oncoming dark-faced hordes;
Was it for this,
To be alone with this button...?

It was all right in the summer, I knew,
But what of the winter, when the steel winds blew?
Then no music sounded for them from gold cages near the sea,
The Promenades were empty.

There, somewhere in this desolate white desert
Of winter houses, pricked by the steel needles of the churches,
Set in a shining waste of pavement,
Major and Mrs. Postlethwaite would sit alone
In their fire-lit tent of tablecloths and white lace curtains.
He fingered the button,
And thought of wooden mansions in the torrid zone,
And silent-footed dusky servants fanning.

But here the wind is cooled by other feathers,
The crystal feathers of the snow,
And one day, sweeping the Promenade,
Where Major Postlethwaite walked to warm himself,
More deft than any Indian sword,
It cut him down and laid him neatly in his coffin –
Just as, when someone calls me and I shut the lid,
His ghost falls,
        Down,
            Down,
                Down
                    Into this box.

Sir Osbert Sitwell (1892–1969)

8

Nell Gwynne's Looking-glass

Glass antique! 'twixt thee and Nell
Draw we here a parallel.
She, like thee, was forced to bear
All reflections, foul or fair.

Thou art deep and bright within, –
Depths as bright belonged to Gwynne;
Thou art very frail as well,
Frail as flesh is – so was Nell.

L. Blanchard

9

The Treasure Box

Ann in chill moonlight unlocks
Her polished brassbound treasure-box,
Draws a soft breath, prepares to spread
The toys around her on the bed.
She dips for luck: by luck pulls out
A silver pig with ring in snout,
The sort that Christmas puddings yield;
Next comes a painted nursery shield
Boy-carved; and then two yellow gloves,
A Limerick wonder that Ann loves,
Leather so thin and joined so well
The pair fold in a walnut shell;
Here's patchwork that her sister made
With antique silk and flower brocade,
Small faded scraps in memory rich
Joined each to each with feather-stitch;
Here's cherry and forget-me-not
Ribbon bunched in a great knot;
A satin purse with pansies on it;
A Tudor baby's christening bonnet;
Old Mechlin lace minutely knit
(Some women's eyes went blind for it):
And Spanish broideries that pinch
Three blossomed rose-trees to one inch;
Here are Ann's brooches, simple pins,
A Comet brooch, two Harlequins,
A Posy; here's a great resplendent
Dove-in-bush Italian pendant;
A Chelsea gift-bird; a toy whistle;
A halfpenny stamped with the Scots thistle;
A Breguet watch; a coral string;
Her mother's thin-worn wedding ring;
A straw box full of hard smooth sweets;
A book, the *Poems of John Keats*;
A chessman; a pink paper rose;
A diary dwindling to its close
Nine months ago; a worsted ball;
A patchbox; a stray match – that's all,

All but a few small treasured scraps
Of paper; things forbid perhaps –
See how slowly Ann unties
The packet where her heartache lies;
Watch her lips move; she slants a letter
Up towards the moon to read it better
(The moon may master what he can).
R stands for Richard, A for Ann,
And L... at this the old moon blinks
And softly from the window shrinks.

Robert Graves (1895–1985)

10

To Richard Boyle, Earl of Burlington

'Tis strange, the miser should his cares employ
To gain those riches he can ne'er enjoy:
Is it less strange, the prodigal should waste
His wealth to purchase what he can ne'er taste?
Not for himself he sees, or hears, or eats;
Artists must choose his pictures, music, meats:
He buys for Topham[1] drawings and designs,
For Pembroke statues, dirty gods and coins;[2]
Rare monkish manuscripts for Hearne alone,
And books for Mead, and butterflies for Sloane.[3]
Think we all these are for himself? no more
Than his fine wife, alas! or finer whore.

His study! with what authors is it stored?
In books, not authors, curious is my lord;
To all their dated backs he turns you round;
These Aldus printed, those Du Sueil has bound.
Lo, some are vellum, and the rest as good,
For all his lordship knows, but they are wood.
For Locke or Milton 'tis in vain to look,
These shelves admit not any modern book.

Alexander Pope (1688–1744)

[1] A well-known collector of paintings.
[2] Thomas, eighth Earl of Pembroke, who collected
the statues and medals at Wilton.
[3] Two eminent physicians: one had an excellent
library, the other the finest collection in Europe of
natural curiosities. Dr. Mead's books consisted of
about 10,000 volumes which, with his valuable
collection of medals and paintings, were sold by
auction after his death in 1754. The collection of
Sir Hans Sloane, who died in 1753, became the
nucleus of the British Museum.

11

A Persian Mirror Case

'But stay! you're known as a connoisseur,
I'm nothing but a hunter; let me have
Your frank opinion of these curios;
A few of them, perhaps, almost excuse
My youthful passion for discarded faiths:
Some even have made converts, so beware!' –

He watched me half-amused, half-anxiously,
As I began to finger souvenirs
Of worn-out empires; marbles; amulets
Of pearl and jade fantastically shaped:
Intaglios; hunting-scenes in miniature,
Turban and tester on a ground of gold;
Bejewelled daggers, blades of damascene.
My hand was on a sword-hilt as he said: –
'Tradition has it, that was Baber's once,
The founder of the Mogul dynasty;
A small thing set to inches, but in craft
It dwarfs the roof-tops of the skyscraper.'
Thereon I turned to scrutinize the head
Of a white Arab carved in ivory,
With studded turquoises for caparison...

But now my wandering eye was called to halt
By a small object I had half mistook
For some old manuscript: a painted case.
Unceremoniously I took it up
To turn toward the light; was ill-content,
Not knowing why; the shadows seemed to cleave,
To nurse it, to pursue; hoar memories
Came with them, vaguely, as a summer mist
Lets just the tallest tree-tops pierce through.
'This has the quality,' I said in muse,
'Of certain of the Umbrian primitives;
Directness, feeling, far beyond the reach
Of any copyist; I'd like to know
Its story.' Laughing he rejoined: – 'You shall.
It's worth the telling. It's a mirror-case,

Well-suited to the nomad, of a kind
Much prized as keepsakes in Safavi days:
The tones, you see, are fresh as Memling's own.
It came to me by way of gratitude
From one of royal descent; it so befell
I proved of service to him in the chase;
An incident, no more; but he was loud
In thanks, insisted I had saved his life;
He wouldn't even speak of recompense,
He was too deeply in my debt, he could
But ask acceptance of a token, one
Much treasured: it had been a nuptial gift
Made to Shah Abbas, his great ancestor,
Best and most famous of a line of kings,
Dearest to Persian legend.' On essay
To open it, he added, – 'It is sealed.'
'What! A mere mirror? Surely the whole worth
Lies in the painting?' – 'As a frontispiece.
But look once more; look as a saint might look,
Or as a lover; not for fleck or flaw,
Not in appraisal, but as waiting spring.'

I made my mind obedient to his wish.
Across the azure, overhanging all,
Wide stretched an almond tree, with breaking bud.
Beneath it was a well, and sitting there
A girl with unfilled pitcher; just a girl!..
How many others gathered day by day
To fill their pitchers! Answered the first call!
Love comes to them like pollen on the wind;
They meet; they mate; they sorrow; they forget.
But here was one who waited; suitors came
And went; some casual, some insistent; still
She waited on; her eyes had caught the trick
Of buried waters: eyes that wooed and warned,
That haunted and caressed; the eyes of fate.
'You wonder even now, at the dead mask!
That pitcher-girl became Shah Abbas' queen!
And at the bridals stepped her uncle forth,
A Mage held high in honour, with these words: –
"I bear a message from the Lord of Light,
A symbol of his monarchy; behold!
Here are two pictures: one, Meraz the fair;
Her heart is thine ten times a thousand suns;
The temple doves have taught her how to breathe
Sweet counsel; shaded rivers are her locks;

Her eyes the onyxes in Ormund's crown.
Open: thou seest the mirror of thine heart
Lest time bedim it look thereon each morn,
And thou shalt prosper like a breaking rose
On Kirman's heights; forbear, and soon thy throne
Shall be a sandhill circling in the wind,
The seat of vultures, the repair of wolves.
Mithra hath spoken: King of Kings, give ear." –
To which in humble gravity the king: –
"I love this maiden as I love my life;
Henceforth they're one; nor tide nor tomb shall part;
This mirror be my daily witnesser;
May darkness cloud it if I prove untrue." –
For forty years the dromedary plied
With silk and spice from Tabriz to Kabul;
The jackal starved; the caravansary
Was flocked with travellers; for forty years
The waters of Karun were dark with freights
Of dropping gum and piled pistachio;
Rich tribute came from snowy Nishapur
To the sun-palace; Kasham toiled in peace;
Where once the slopes ran blood in Kirmanshah,
Waved peach and prunus and pomegranate-bloom
Gold lay the grain-fields; unmolested went
The husbandman to bind his stooping sheaves,
And the Kurd shepherd trod Urmia's bank
As softly as the stars; for forty years
The songs of Hafiz lived on wooers' lips,
And Jami's tales held night a listener.
Then Abbas died, and with him died the light
Of Persia; with him the dove-voices died;
No lattices kept watch in Isphahan:
The courts were strangely still, no citherns sang,
No bulbuls answered! but the tamarisks
Were trampled by the wild-ass in his flight.
As for this marriage-gift of Abbas's queen.
Succeeding lustrums saw it handed on
From prince to prince, unsceptred each by each,
None heeding it; perhaps none dared regard;
For cruelty, callous in commission, still
Is awed at its own soul.' –

He paused as though
His very words had taken fright. And there,
Between us, part in sunlight, part in shade,
Still lay the picture, stretched the almond-tree.

To urge him to fresh speech I commented: –
'One gap needs filling to round off your tale.
The mirror's hid. Wherefore? I comprehend
That the same temper which will snatch a throne
May pause at some slight act inconsequent
To which tradition has attached a fear;
I liked your cabbala: it has the breath
Of summer greatness, though in truth it owed
Whatever potency it once possessed
To priestcraft playing upon ignorance:
But since the dynasty that gave it birth,
Strange ears have heard it: no respect belongs
To threats unsocketed; to leave the seal
Almost attacks the owner.' 'You mistake.'
'Others have seen it, then?' – 'A score, perhaps,
Since my return.' – 'And found strange visions there?' –
'Their bearing shows it; women even swoon.' –
'That's not a cause for wonder; there are minds
That stuff a painted tale with shreds of fact
And make it their own scarecrow.' – 'You mistake;
No-one has heard the story till this hour.
Children see nothing there; the bravest blench,
The timidest are proof; age, arrogance
Are its worst subjects; shrewd men set it down
As though some fabled gem had slipped their grasp
Of which they once had glimpses.' – 'Pray unseal,
And give the Persian wizard a last chance
To show his power. For me, a heaven lost
Is better than no heaven; rivers old
And sad, long gone to sea, still leave a train
Of echoes in the wilted willow-tree.' –
'Prove me at fault, then: so you'll please me best:
Ho! Sesame!' –

At first, as in a trance,
The fascination of the pitcher-girl
Was still before me: flowers and hair and eyes;
The gazing on her, so I told myself,
Had fooled the senses; then they slowly took
New shades, new shapes. The almond-blossom paled
To a wild cherry waking at the touch
Of the spring breezes, the deep curtained well
Spread like a fan until a rounded pool,
Asleep in the new bracken, lapped my feet;
The pitcher was a knoll whereon there rose
Tall firs, as red as fire, with sable crowns;

I walked beneath them and the woodpeckers
Dipped laughingly away. My heart laughed too;
The sunbeams laughed, and all the buttercups
Rocked with light laughter. Yet another dawn,
And there'll be reaping; comings to and fro;
Rough swink and sweat; the glory'll be gone;
Now all's expentancy. This is the day
When every meadow is in full attire,
When every bud has burst, no petal fallen,
No branches bowed; this is the one pure day
That all the birds have brought from all fair skies,
That comes with them o'ernight and makes the world
A living flame; like flighting birds it comes.

James Elroy Flecker (1884–1915)

12

A Likeness

Some people hang portraits up
In a room where they dine or sup:
And the wife clinks tea-things under,
And her cousin, he stirs his cup,
Asks, 'Who was the lady, I wonder?'
''Tis a daub John bought at a sale,'
Quoth the wife, – looks black as thunder:
'What a shade beneath her nose!'
'Snuff-taking, I suppose, –'
Adds the cousin, while John's corns ail.
Or else, there's no wife in the case,
But the portrait's queen of the place,
Alone 'mid the other spoils
Of youth, – masks, gloves and foils,
And pipe-sticks, rose, cherry-tree, jasmine,
And the long whip, the tandem-lasher,
And the cast from a fist ('not, alas! mine,
But my master's, the Tipton Slasher'),
And the cards where pistol-balls mark ace,
And a satin shoe used for cigar-case,
And the chamois-horns ('shot in the Chablais')
And prints – Rarey drumming on Cruiser,
And Sayers, our champion, the bruiser,
And the little edition of Rabelais:
Where a friend, with both hands in his pockets,
May saunter up close to examine it,
And remark a good deal of Jane Lamb in it,
'But the eyes are half out of their sockets;
'That hair's not so bad, where the gloss is,
'But they've made the girl's nose a proboscis:
'Jane Lamb, that we danced with at Vichy!
'What, is not she Jane? Then, who is she?'

All that I own is a print,
An etching, a mezzotint;
'Tis a study, a fancy, a fiction,
Yet a fact (take my conviction)
Because it has more than a hint
Of a certain face, I never
Saw elsewhere touch or trace of
In women I've seen the face of:
Just an etching, and, so far, clever.

I keep my prints, an imbroglio,
Fifty in one portfolio.
When somebody tries my claret,
We turn round chairs to the fire,
Chirp over days in a garret,
Chuckle o'er increase of salary,
Taste the good fruits of our leisure,
Talk about pencil and lyre,
And the National Portrait Gallery:
Then I exhibit my treasure.

After we've turned over twenty,
And the debt of wonder my crony owes,
Is paid to my Marc Antonios,
He stops me – '*Festina lentè*!
'What's that sweet thing there, the etching?'
How my waistcoat-strings want stretching,
How my cheeks grow red as tomatos,
How my heart leaps! But hearts, after leaps, ache.

'By the by, you must take, for a keepsake,
'That other, you praised, of Volpato's.'
The fool! would he try a flight further and say –
He never saw, never before to-day,
What was able to take his breath away,
A face to lose youth for, to occupy age
With the dream of, meet death with, – why,
I'll not engage
But that, half in a rapture and half in a rage,
I should toss him the thing's self – ''Tis only
a duplicate,
'A thing of no value! Take it, I supplicate!'

George Colman the Younger (1762–1836)

13

The Collector to his Library

Brown books of mine, who never yet
Have caused me anguish or regret, –
Save when some fiend in human shape
Has set your tender sides agape.
Or soiled with some unmanly smear
The candour of your margin clear,
Or writ you with some phrase inane,
The bantling of an idle brain, –
I love you: and because must end
The commerce between friend and friend,
I do implore each kindly Fate –
To each and all I supplicate –
That you, whom I have loved so long
May not be vended 'for a song'; –
That you, my dear desire and care,
May 'scape the common thoroughfare,
The dust, the eating rain, and all
The shame and squalor of the Stall.
Rather I trust your lot may touch
Some Croesus – if there should be such –
To buy you, and that you may so
From Croesus unto Croesus go
Till that inevitable day
When comes your moment of decay.

This, more than other good, I pray.

Austin Dobson (1840–1921)

14

Fenders

'Fenders,' the man in the Bond Street shop
With the very slight lisp opined,
'Fenders of any quality
Are most terribly hard to find.
We very rarely get them
And we never have them long;
Now this is a pretty specimen
Of early Ting-Tsai-Wong.'

'The point,' I replied, 'is this, 'tis I
Who have a fender available,
And if, as you say, fine fenders
Are as scarce as they are saleable,
It follows (as the winter
Does the autumn) that my fender
Should fetch a price approximately
Worthy of its splendour.'

'Ah', said the man in the Bond Street shop,
'Of course, we'd have to see it.
If it is screwed on the floor of course
We would need a man to free it.
It might be too short or too long of course,
And it might have to go to the mender.
And we'd charge you a moderate fee of course
To tender for your fender.

'It's bound to be too severe you know,
If it's not too ornamental.
Is the motif somewhat oppressive
Or if anything too gentle?
No doubt it's a splendid fender
And your asking price is a gift
But they are so easy to come by
And difficult to shift.'

'But my fender,' I said, 'is perfection.
It is not too short or long
And it's just the same to look at
As your piece of Ting-Tsai-Wong.'
'Sir,' said the man in the Bond Street shop,
'I am sure they are sister and brother
But as I can't sell this one,
What on *earth* would I do with another?'

Alistair Sampson (1929–2006)

15

To a Graven Image

Thou that on me and all thou canst espy
Dost glare with baleful and malignant eye,
That since thy coming has beset me still
With wizard arts to work my household ill,
Till morns successive new misfortunes bring –
Abate thy spite, unreasonable Thing!
Accept thy lot: from dull resentment cease;
And sit contented on my mantelpiece!

I know the cause: I know thou wouldst prefer
The peace of that Egyptian sepulchre
Wherefrom thou wast incontinently hurled
Into the tumults of an alien world; –
What's done is done; thou canst not always have
The calm and darkness of that distant grave:
Brief is our span, philosophers have said:
Life waits for all – you can't be always dead.
There where they set thee in the silent ring
Of carven slaves who watched their buried king,
There where thou didst for age on age repose,
While empires fell and other empires rose,
Strangers have come: Research hath cancelled quite
Thy long, long lease of immemorial night:
The unhallowed lamp of artificial day
Illumes the darkness where thy monarch lay:
Far, far from home thy lord embalmèd lies,
A K-nyon's treasure or a P-trie's prize:
The grave is rifled and the shrine is bare –
Nor slave nor Pharaoh can inhabit there.
Relax thy look of concentrated gloom!
It was not I that took thee from the tomb;
The mounds of Memphis and of Meroe
Know countless robbers, but they know not me;
Not mine to mar with sacrilegious spade
Sakkara's sands or Gizeh's haunted shade;
Nay, hear the truth: the facts I will declare;
Thou wast at Cairo and I found thee there, –
I found thee there 'mid trophies of the grave,

Exposed for sale like any other slave,
For sale exposed 'mid mere unpurchased lots –
Suspected scarabs and imperfect pots; –
There (though I might by kinder fortune led
Have bought a scarab or a pot instead)
I, not divining thy ingratitude,
Thy beastly temper, thy vindictive mood,
I paid the price that thou wast valued at,
('Twas ten piastres, and too much at that;
Alas! what ills from deeds of mercy come!)
I bought thy freedom and I took thee home.

Change then thy spells: or thou shalt straightway go
(Bear witness, Isis! that the fact is so)
'Mid Ashmole's hoards to play a humbler part
As paltry rubbish (which, in truth, thou art);
There, while Professors of a mightier charm
Mock and contemn thy petty powers to harm,
There shalt thou lie on some neglected shelf
And learn the value of thy worthless self!

Alfred Denis Godley (1856–1925)

16

On Looking at Stubbs's Anatomy of the Horse

In Lincolnshire, a village full of tongues
Not tired by a year's wagging, and a man
Shut in a room where a wrecked carcass hangs,
His calm knife peeling putrid flesh from bone.
He whistles softly, as an ostler would;
The dead horse moves, as if it understood.

That night a yokel holds the taproom still
With tales new-hatched; he's peeped, and seen a mare
Stand there alive with naked rib and skull –
The creature neighed, and stamped upon the floor;
The warlock asked her questions, and she spoke;
He wrote her answers down in a huge book.

Two centuries gone, I have the folio here,
And turn the pages, find them pitiless,
These charts of sinew, vein and bone require
A glance more expert, more detached than this –
Fingering the margins, I think of the old
Sway-backed and broken nags the pictures killed.

Yet, standing in that room, I watch the knife;
Light dances on it as it maps a joint
Or scribes a muscle; I am blank and stiff
The blade cuts so directly to my want;
I gape for anecdote, absurd detail,
Like any yokel with his pint of ale.

Edward Lucie-Smith (1933–)

17

To the Pliocene Skull
(A Geological Address)

'Speak, O man, less recent! Fragmentary fossil!
Primal pioneer of pliocene formation,
Hid in lowest drifts below the earliest stratum
 Of volcanic tufa!

'Older than the beasts, the oldest Palaeotherium;
Older than the trees, the oldest Cryptogami;
Older than the hills, those infantile eruptions
Of earth's epidermis!

'Eo-Mio-Plio-whatsoe'er the "cene" was
That those vacant sockets filled with awe and wonder, –
Whether shores Devonian or Silurian beaches, –
Tell us thy strange story!

'Or has the professor slightly antedated
By some thousand years thy advent on this planet,
Giving thee an air that's somewhat better fitted
For cold-blooded creatures?

'Wert thou true spectator of that mighty forest
When above thy head the stately Sigillaria
Reared its columned trunks in that remote and distant
Carboniferous epoch?

'Tell us of that scene, – the dim and watery woodland,
Songless, silent, hushed, with never bird or insect,
Veiled with spreading fronds and screened with tall clubmosses,
Lycopodiacea, –

'When beside thee walked the solemn Plesiosaurus,
And around thee crept the festive Ichthyosaurus,
While from time to time above thee flew and circled
Cheerful Pterodactyls.

'Tell us of thy food, – those half-marine refections,
Crinoids on the shell and Brachipods *au naturel*, –
Cuttlefish to which the *pieuvre* of Victor Hugo
Seems a periwinkle.

'Speak, thou awful vestige of the earth's creation, –
Solitary fragment of remains organic!
Tell the wondrous secret of thy past existence, –
Speak! thou oldest primate!'

Even as I gazed, a thrill of the maxilla,
And a lateral movement of the condyloid process,
With post-pliocene sounds of healthy mastication,
Ground the teeth together.

And, from that imperfect dental exhibition,
Stained with express juices of the weed Nicotian,
Came these hollow accents, blent with softer murmurs
Of expectation:

'Which my name is Bowers, and my crust was busted
Falling down a shaft in Calaveras County,
But I'd take it kindly if you'd send the pieces
Home to old Missouri!'

Bret Harte (1836–1902)

18

Of Taste (1756)

Of late, 'tis true, quite sick of Rome and Greece
We fetch our models from the wise Chinese;
European artists are too cool and chaste,
For Mand'rin is the only man of taste ...
On ev'ry shelf a Joss divinely stares,
Nymphs laid on chintzes sprawl upon our chairs;
While o'er our cabinets Confucius nods,
Midst porcelain elephants and China gods.

James Cawthorn (1719–1761)

19

A Dealer Visits

There isn't a thing in the house, you know,
That's what you would call 'old';
Except this little inkstand here,
We rather think it's gold.

It's really quite a work of art.
Such work is in the legs –
And those stains inside the ink-pot,
They're the original dregs.

You see those feathers at the back?
That's called a *fleur-de-lis*.
I wouldn't sell it for the world,
Though I wish I knew its price.

Alistair Sampson (1929–2006)

20

Laocoön

From heaped-up mound of earth and from the heart
Of mighty ruins, lo! long time once more
Has brought Laocoön home, who stood of old
In princely palaces and graced thy halls,
Imperial Titus. Wrought by skill divine
(Even learned ancients saw no nobler work),
The statue now from darkness saved returns
To see the stronghold of Rome's second life.

Cardinal Sadoleto

(The Elder Pliny, shortly before his death in AD 79, noted in his *Natural History* a famous statue – 'The Laocoön, which stands in the palace of the Emperor Titus, a work to be preferred to all that the arts of painting and sculpture have produced. Out of one block of stone the consummate artists, Agesandros, Poludoros, and Athenodoros of Rhodes made, after careful planning, Laocoön, his sons, and the snakes marvellously entwined about them.'

The group, perhaps a Roman copy of a Hellenistic work of the second century BC, represents the punishment of Laocoön, Apollo's disobedient priest at Troy, crushed, with his sons, by monstrous serpents sent by the angry god.

After Pliny's reference, fourteen centuries elapsed. Then, in 1506, a Roman gentleman named de Fredis, digging out old walls in his vineyard near the Baths of Trajan and probably in the buried rooms of Nero's Golden House, came upon this marble comparatively undamaged. It was recognized at once from Pliny's description, and Julius II claimed it for the papal collection. Michelangelo, among others, examined it. It had a big influence on later sculptors. The latest theory is that Michelangelo carved it as a hoax!)

21

Homage to the British Museum

There is a Supreme God in the ethnological section;
A hollow toad shape, faced with a blank shield.
He needs his belly to include the Pantheon,
Which is inserted through a hole behind.
At the navel, at the points formally stressed, at the organs of sense,
Lice glue themselves, dolls, local deities,
His smooth wood creeps with all the creeds of the world.

Attending there let us absorb the cultures of nations
And dissolve into our judgement all their codes.
Then, being clogged with a natural hesitation
(People are continually asking one the way out).
Let us stand here and admit that we have no road.
Being everything, let us admit that is to be something,
Or give ourselves the benefit of the doubt;
Let us offer our pinch of dust all to this God,
And grant his reign over the entire building.

William Empson (1906–84)

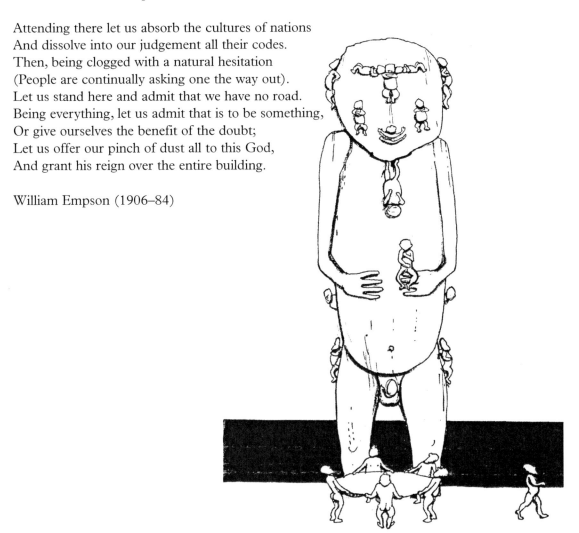

22

An Old Fan (To Kitty, Her Reverie)

It is soiled and quite *passé*,
Broken, too, and out of fashion,
But it stirs my heart some way,
As I hold it here today,
With a dead year's grave and passion.
Oh, my pretty fan!

Precious dreams and thrilling strain,
Rise up from that vanished season;
Back to heart and nerve and brain
Sweeps the joy as keen as pain,
Joy that asks no cause or reason,
Oh, my dainty fan!

Hopes that perished in a night
Gaze at me like spectral faces;
Grim despair and lost delight,
Sorrow long since gone from sight –
All are hiding in these laces.
Oh, my broken fan!

Let us lay the thing away –
I am sadder now and older;
Fled the ballroom and the play –
You have had your foolish day,
And the night and life are colder.
Exit – little fan!

Ella Wheeler Wilcox (1850–1919)

23

Mr. Battoni's Collection

On the whole, Mrs. Battoni
Liked what Signor Battoni collected –
That is, she liked the antiques
But not the young girls.

Sir Osbert Sitwell (1892–1969)

24

The Antiquary

When days begin to lengthen oot
At seed-time o' the year,
A wee bald-heided cratur, stoot,
Wi' glasses on, comes here.
It's sic a sure and sartin fack
That lengthenin's days will bring
Our frien' the antiquary back,
He's ca'd 'the Sign o' Spring.'
He'll scart auld tombstanes by the 'oor
To find some name or date,
His face a' blacken'd by the stour, –
What cares he? – deil a haet.
He revels in blue-mowlded things
That mickle need a wash,
Auld rusty buckles, bolts, and rings,
That common folk ca' trash.
For twa-three fussils frae a rock
He'll walk ten mile or mair;
H'd gie his heid for some auld crock
O' prehistoric ware.
The bits o' trumpery he brings
Up by to let me see
Are juist the maist rediklus things
That's possible to be.
He's got the veritable tail
O' Queen Matilda's sark,
The jug that used to haud the ale
That Shakspere drank at wark;
He's got the tawse King David used
To scalp unruly weans,
And twa pair breeches, much abus'd
That cloth'd his nether banes;
The circlet o' Queen Mary's waist
(A dirty-lookin' dud),
The tail hairs o' an anshent baste
That leev'd before the flood.
A these and muckle mair I've seen –
Things brocht frae every airt;

Let but the thing be auld, my frien'
Will tak' it to his hairt.

I mind me o' the day when first
I met him wi' his load;
The horse had stopp'd to quench his thirst
As he cam' doon the road.
He emptied oot his bag o'stanes
On paper on his knees,
And show'd me some wi' herrin'-banes
And some wi' marks likc trees.
'Are only ammonites,' quo' he,
'In these pairts roundabout?'
I thocht he pokit fun at me
And answered straight: 'Nae doot
There's lots o' them – they're common sights,
Ye'll fin' them here in wheens,
And Jebusites and Moabites
And sometimes Philistines.'

I had nae lear o' fossils then,
Nor ever had a squint
At tools o' prehistoric men.
Or workit flake o' flint.
But ere he left I thocht I knew
A guid deal o' the trade,
And thocht I understandit hoo
A trifle micht be made.
He read me frae his catalogues
The price o' flints and stanes,
The horns o' animals frae bogs,
Auld skulls, and bits o' banes.
It seemit strange that folk should buy
Sic ugly, useless trash,
But if they wantit it – why, I
Wad find it them – for cash.

Next morn I started to colleck,
And drew a load o' flint;
I had, as near's I recolleck,
Five thoosan' pieces in't.
I valued them at twopence each,
'Twas naethin' to the price
That larn'd professor folk wha teach
Wad fork out in a trice.
I fun' twa useless kitchen crooks,

A braukin three-legg'd pot,
Some rusty spades and reapin' hooks,
And for the anshent lot
I fixed a guinea to be paid
Sae moderate was I;
Auld airn work my frien' had said
Museum folk wad buy.
I minded me my feyther's dog,
He had when we were weans,
Was deid and berrit in the bog –
I diggit up the banes.
I pric'd the skull at one pun' ten,
Leg banes ten shillin' each;
No' willin' that the teacher men
Shaid fin' them oot o' reach.
The shafts o' an auld rotten cairt
And keel o' fishin' boat,
I thocht, self-interest apairt,
Were worth a five-pun' note.

My treasures a' by Monday night
Were rangit in a row,
They seemed to my unlearnit sight
To mak' a guidly show.
The chairge, too, seemed a proper fee,
But, by the Tuesday morn,
I thocht if but advanced a wee
'Twould buy a field o'corn.
On Wednesday I thocht the price
Was still a bit too low;
It should, at varra laste, be twice
As much – I made it so.
Thinks I at that I'll let it be,
From addin' mair refrain;
By Friday afternoon at three
I raised the price again.
I thocht wi' guid museum stuff
Anither rise nae hairm;
By Saturday I had enough
To buy a dacent fairm.

And then my thochts went far afield,
And saw a bright career;
If yin sma' week a' that can yield
What winna dae a year?
Ye ken hoo thocht desires will breed

And hoo desires expand;
A farm nae langer satisfeed,
I bocht the haill toon-land.
And noo a person o' estate
Wi' lands let oot on lease,
I saw mysel' a magistrate,
A justice o' the peace.
Sae verra near and sure it seem'd,
My bosom heav'd wi' pride;
I leeved respeckit and esteem'd
By a' the country side.

Next week my frien' a veesit paid,
We clamber'd straight abaft
To whaur my precious stock in trade
Was rangit in the laft.
I show'd wi' ill-concealit glee
The objecks o' my quest,
He look'd at them – he look'd at me, –
I needna tell the rest.

John Stevenson

25

Mr. Goodbeare's Parlour

Mr. Goodbeare's parlour was a paradise
Of polished wood, a haven of varnish.
There were brackets, shelves, shields
And cupboards, with ferns traced on them
By his artistry,
And even wooden vases, turned
So beautifully, and full of dried, dull grasses,
Tied with dusty ribbons,
That rustled suffocatingly
In the dry wind from under the door.
Fantastic flights of Mr. Goodbeare's imagination,
Cricket-bats combined with dragons,
And improbable bows and loops,
Framed-in the almost legendary
Topiary of beard and whisker –
Tied in True-Lovers Knots,
In which Mr. Goodbeare's friends
Had at one time extravagantly –
If elegantly – indulged.

Sir Osbert Sitwell (1892–1969)

26

Ozymandias (1818)

I met a traveller from an antique land
Who said: Two vast and trunkless legs of stone
Stand in the desert ... Near them, on the sand,
Half sunk, a shattered visage lies, whose frown,
And wrinkled lip, and sneer of cold command,
Tell that its sculptor well those passions read
Which yet survive, stamped on these lifeless things,
The hand that mocked them, and the heart that fed:
And on the pedestal these words appear:
'My name is Ozymandias, king of kings:
Look on my works, ye Mighty, and despair!'
Nothing beside remains. Round the decay
Of that colossal wreck, boundless and bare
The lone and level sands stretch far away.

Percy Bysshe Shelley (1792–1822)

27

Precious Stones
An Incident in Modern History

My Cherrystones! I prize them,
No tongue can tell how much!
Each lady caller eyes them,
And madly longs to touch!
At eve I lift them down, I look
Upon them, and I cry;
Recalling how my Prince 'partook'
(Sweet word!) of cherry-pie!

To me it was an Era
In life, that Déjeuner!
They ate, they sipp'd Madeira
Much in the usual way.
Many a soft item there would be,
No doubt, upon the carte:
But one made life a heaven to me:
It was the cherry-tart.

Lightly the spoonfuls enter'd
That mouth on which the gaze
Of ten fine girls was centred
In rapturous amaze.
Soon that august assemblage clear'd
The dish; and – as they ate –
The stones, all coyly, re-appeared
On each illustrious plate.

And when His Royal Highness
Withdrew to take the air,
Waiving our natural shyness,
We swoop'd upon his chair.
Policemen at our garments clutch'd:
We mock'd those feeble powers;
And soon the treasures that had touch'd
Exalted lips were ours!

Our large one – at the moment
It seem'd almost divine –
Was got by that Miss Beaumont:
And three, O three, are mine!
Yes! the three stones that rest beneath
Glass, on that plain deal shelf,
Stranger, once dallied with the teeth
Of Royalty itself.

Let Parliament abolish
Churches and States and Thrones:
With reverent hand I'll polish
Still, still my Cherrystones!
A clod – a piece of orange-peel
An end of a cigar –
Once trod on by a Princely heel,
How beautiful they are!

Years since, I climb'd Saint Michael
His Mount: – you'll all go there
Of course, and those who like'll
Sit in Saint Michael's Chair:
For there I saw, within a frame,
The pen – O heavens! the pen –
With which a Duke had sign'd his name,
And other gentlemen.

'Great among geese,' I faltered,
'Is she who grew that quill!'
And, Deathless Bird, unalter'd
Is mine opinion still.
Yet sometimes, as I view my three
Stones with a thoughtful brow,
I think there possibly might be
E'en greater geese than thou.

Charles Stuart Calverley (1831–84)

HRH ᴛʜᴇ PRINCE
ᴏꜰ WALES

28

On Seeing an Arm'd Bust of the King of Prussia Curiously Imprinted on a Porcelain Cup of the Worcester Manufacture, with the Emblems of his Victories. Inscribed to Mr. Josiah Holdship

Here, taught by thee, we view with raptured eyes,
Graceful and bold, the Prussian hero rise –
The royal chief, the Caesar of his age,
Whose acts the wonder of the world engage.
The martial spirit animates his mien,
His heart intrepid, and his look serene.
There Fame, regardless else who reigns or bleeds,
With all her breath resounds his mighty deeds.
Here from whole nations in the field o'erthrown,
He points to trophies which are all his own;
While Victory gives to valour so renown'd
The blooming wreath which her own temples bound.

See where his virtues still his life expose,
And smile defiance to surrounding foes.
The intriguing Saxon see him there[4] surprise;
Here from his arms the Imperial Eagle[5] flies;
Tho' fortune frowns,[6] unknowing how to yield,
He drives, by proxy, Russia from the field.
Now, farther prest, behold him still advance,
And pour destruction on the troops[7] of France;
Before his glitt'ring arms the Swedes retire,
And mourn pale Envy's unfulfilled desire.
Yet lo! once more by frowning fortune crost,
He sees a battle, Breslau, Bevern lost:

[4] At Pirna.
[5] The battle of Prague.
[6] The battle with Ct. Daun, 18th of June.
[7] The battle with the Prince Soubise, November 3.

Yet soon, that loss retrieved, the hero gains
Immortal glory on Silesian plains.
His active spirit still disdains repose,
Resolv'd to combat with stern wintry snows;
And through the regions of her cold domain,
To stretch the triumphs of the long campaign.
What praise, ingenious HOLDSHIP, is thy due,
Who first on porcelain the fair portrait drew;
Who first alone to full perfection brought
The curious art, by rival numbers sought.
Hence shall thy skill inflame heroic souls,
Who mighty battles see round mightier bowls;
While Albion's sons shall see their features, name,
And actions copied on the cup of fame.

Hence beauty, which repairs the waste of war,
Beauty may triumph on a china jar:
And this, perhaps, with stronger faith to trust,
Than the stain'd canvas or the marble bust.
For here, who once in youthful charms appears
May bloom uninjured for a thousand years;

May time – till now opposed in vain – defie,
And live still fair, till Nature's self shall die.
Here may the toasts of every age be seen,
From Britain's Gunning back to Sparta's Queen;
And every hero history's page can bring
From Macedonia's down to Prussia's king.

Perhaps the art may track the circling world,
Where'er thy Britain has her sails unfurl'd;
While wond'ring *China* shall with envy see,
And stoop to borrow her own arts from thee.

CYNTHIO. Worcester, 20th Dec, 1757.

The above poem appeared in the *Gentleman's Magazine* for December 1757. A different version was printed in the *Worcester Journal* of January 1758, with the addition of a couplet, an '*extempore* on the compliment of imprinting the King of Prussia's Bust being ascribed to Mr Josiah Holdship'. The *extempore* was as follows:

Handcock, my friend, don't *grieve*, tho' Holdship has the praise,
'Tis yours to execute – 'tis his to wear the bays.

And indeed the 'King of Prussia' (ie Frederick the Great) mugs transfer-printed at Worcester bore the initials of Robert Hancock, who executed the design.
Carlyle mentions such a mug, in his usual declamatory style, in his *Frederick the Great*.

29

A Squire's Taste

His mansion was the pink of taste and art,
His charming pictures! oh, how they delighted you!
In his saloon Egyptian monsters frighted you,
And pagods on his staircase made you start.

Nothing surpassed his carpets and his draperies,
His clocks, chairs, tables, sofas, ottomans;
His rooms were crowded with Etruscan aperies,
Fine noseless busts, and Roman pots and pans.

He had a marble Venus on a stand,
Wanting a leg and a right hand;
A sweeter piece of art was never found;
Had not those brutes, the sailors, rot 'em!
In bringing her from Rome knock'd off her bottom,
She would have sold for thirty thousand pound.
His candlesticks, when guests retired to beds,
Were Cleopatras splashed with ormolu,
Or squab Mark Antonies, antiquely new,
With wax-lights rammed into their hands or heads.

In every bedroom there were placed
Knick-knackeries of wondrous taste,
With shells, and spars, stuffed birds, and flies in amber;
And by the side of every bed
There stood a Grecian urn instead
Of what is called in France a *pot-de-chambre*.
To see the wonders of a house thus stocked,
His London friends in shoals came down,
Though he resided sixty miles from town,
And parties upon parties flocked.

Now they who came these vanities to view
Did not care twopence for virtu;
Nor for the dwelling, nor the dweller;
But they delighted very much to look
On the rare *carre*-work of the squire's French cook,
And to inspect, with special care,
Those *crusted vessels*, dragged to air,
From the great *Herculaneum*, his cellar.

George Colman the Elder (1732–94)

30

The Heavenly Swindle

I bought this charming little vase
In one of Auntie's church bazaars.
Lady Bromley-Chumley-Fry
Asked me why I didn't buy
The pretty piece of porcelain
Before the rain came on again.
'It was,' she said, 'a splendid cause,'
And crowned my purchase with applause.
'Ten bob,' she said, and blew a kiss.
'The Vicar will be told of this.'
'Will he?' I said, and left the grounds.
The vase is worth ten thousand pounds.

Alistair Sampson (1929–2006)

In the original, published in 1961,
the vase was worth one hundred
pounds. With the late author's assent,
I have made allowance for inflation.

31

An Arab Drinking-cup

Miracle of opalescence!
Rainbow-reaper and quintessence!
Where did you such florets gather,
Luminous as ring-dove's feather,
Lustrous as the teal's?
Did you find them in the delta
Of old Nilus? From no smelter
Could a craftsman ever spin them,
Could a wizard ever win them
From his crucibles.

You have been unnumbered journeys
In the tilt and thrust and tourneys
Between caliph and crusader,
Holy warden and invader,
Knight and saladin;
You have shared the crescent's glory,
You have seen it torn and gory
In the refluent tide of battle
Till you passed with slave and chattel
To the paladin.

On a thousand thousand corses
Suns have set since first you glistened,
To the whinnies of wild horses
Sands uncountable have listened,
Littered with men's bones;
Where are now the bright cuirasses,
Lion and leopard rampant gardant,
Where the spears in serried masses
Set to dauntless hands and ardent,
And loud Victory's tones?

Paean, pageant, all have perished
With their blazonry once cherished,
Beaten bronze from Vulcan's smithy
Bent as lightly as the withy
'Fore the breath of time;
And yet you live down the ages
Unmolested by men's rages,
You, the sport of rosy fingers,
You, the plaything of old singers
As they turned their rhyme.

Say, what warlock, what magician,
Set his seal on your fruition,
That you, frailty's own exemplar,
Have outlived the bravest Templar
With his retinue?
Were they mitred words that blessed you,
Were they lordly lips caressed you
As you left your fires Phoenician
To watch man and his attrition
The dark ages through?

When you pledged him in a morrow
That was born to sword and sorrow,
When you choked his empty curses
As the dust rose round his hearses,
Whose was the sure hand
That held off the wild destroyer?
Far from candle, crib and foyer,
In the bivouac of Berber
Was there some one face could curb a
Conflict lust had fanned?

Did the frail mimosa hear her
As she left their cruel assortal?
Were the tamarisk bushes near her?
To the night-winds, to no mortal
She betrayed her prayer;
Wind and wave were softly calling
In the gold and silver alleys;
Showers of saffron beads were falling
And you caught them in your chalice
From the burdened air.

There are thoughts that come in armour;
At a touch of the discharmer
All the phalanxes are scattered,
All their towers and temples shattered,
All their glory shorn;
There are thoughts as lightly laden
As the footfall of a maiden
Decades gone, and one mimosa,
Softly blowing, brings them closer
Than at glint of morn.

Aught that touches creed or moral,
Making, breaking, like the coral,
Has its bronze or marble token,
Reared to-day, to-morrow broken,
Parchment, palimpsest;
Masking sacrilege with duty
Gaia's ravished of her beauty,
Rocks are rived for brief possession,
Now Ictinus holds his session,
Now iconoclast.

But you serve for no man's hire
Or in palace or in byre,
Gates of iron, be they gilded,
Hold you not, nor walls high builded
With kings' revenues;
Pedantry and pomp are stranger
To you, born a desert ranger,
Far you track from gorgèd city,
Swift to soothe, to quench, to pity,
Pilgrim of the dews.

For you live where pristine gleams are
By the waters of Osiris,
And you know what loves and dreams are,
And the ways of dimpled Iris,
Loves and dreams and stars;
In the dawn old meandering rivers
Bring their gifts of ore and argent,
In the darkness fickle fevers
Trembling cling about your margent,
Dreams and hates and wars.

'Neath the cool of the pomegranate
You have watched the rising planet
Leave her pillars, golden Hesper,
To the muezzin and the vesper,
And the sea's slow psalms
You have heard the wounded lion
Bay to Virgo and Orion
As he dares the whetted hunter
To renew the dread encounter
Ere he seeks his palms.

On the centuries are creeping,
High the desert sands are heaping,
Still from lip to lip you wander,
Though your nectarine men squander,
Still you travel on;
Mirroring each love-lit fancy
With your coloured necromancy,
Trapping fire-flies in your prism,
Pouring balm and holy chrism
On the widow's groan.

Miracle of light and lustre
Where the falling meteors cluster,
Wander down the purple spaces,
Gather in the green oases
Dewdrops for our scars;
Yours the goal of ancient mages,
Desert fires no time assuages,
Desert spaces are your measure,
Dreams and starlight are your treasure,
Dreams, and trains of stars.

James Elroy Flecker (1884–1915)

32

On a Piece of Tapestry

Hold high the woof, dear friends, that we may see
The cunning mixture of its colours rare.
Nothing in nature purposely is fair, –
Her beauties in their freedom disagree;
But here all vivid dyes that garish be.
To that tint mellowed which the sense will bear,
Glow, and not wound the eye that, resting there,
Lingers to feed its gentle ecstasy.
Crimson and purple and all hues of wine,
Saffron and russet, brown and sober green
Are rich the shadowy depths of blue between;
While silver threads with golden intertwine,
To catch the glimmer of a fickle sheen, –
All the long labour of some captive queen.

George Santayana (1863–1952)

33

A Glass Collection

Today I had a big surprise,
Uncle left me eight glass eyes.
He never used the things himself –
He kept them glaring on a shelf.
And champing on the shelf beneath
Were twenty-seven sets of teeth.
He always was the life and soul
Of every party. He would roll
An eye along the floor and shout,

'Archie, yours has fallen out.'
Uncle's eyes were funny hues,
Mottled greens and pretty blues.
The one he slipped in people's drink
Was flecked with palest, palest pink.
He made me promise I would keep
All eight – now would you like a peep?
You would? All right, but do not feel
Them very hard for one is real.

Alistair Sampson (1929–2006)

The original printed version has 'smiling' instead of 'champing'.
I have the late author's authority for this alteration.

34

The Sir Percival David Collection of Chinese Ceramics

They haunt me, Sir Percival's vases, motionless now
as the potters left them be, yet seeming to spin
just beyond reach of time;
more than mere mortal clay.

Who cares if the fussy Qianlong Emperor
inscribed his pedantic verses upon a dish?
Or if a jar's firm body, clothed in glaze –
shoulder to waist to foot –
were fingered languidly by an ageing man?

Pass me instead a bowl where once swirled wine
distilled from the bamboo's leaf
to tempt an old Tang poet, lips to its lip,
his heart too full to smutch a scroll with thought.
Inkstone and brush could wait upon tomorrow,
next week, never perhaps, for visions fade.

They haunt me, Sir Percival's vases: how they spin!
Just beyond grasp of mind;
more than mere mortal clay.

John Mallet (1930–)

35

Lot 96

Lot 96: a brass-rimmed ironwork fender.
It had stood guard for years, where it used to belong,
Over the hearth of a couple who loved tenderly.
Now it will go for a song.

Night upon winter night, as she gossiped with him
Or was silent, he watched the talkative firelight send
Its reflections twittering over that burnished rim
Like a language of world without end.

Death, which unclasped their hearts, dismantled all.
The world they made is as if it had never been true –
That firelit bubble of warmth, serene, magical,
Ageless in form and hue.

Now there stands, dulled in an auction room,
This iron thing – a far too durable irony
Reflecting never a ghost of the lives that illumed it,
No hint of the sacred fire.

This lot was part of their precious bond, almost
A property of its meaning. Here, in the litter
Washed up by death, values are re-assessed
At a nod from the highest bidder.

C. Day Lewis (1904–72)

36

With a Coin from Syracuse

Where is the hand to trace
The contour of her face:
The nose so straight and fine
Down from the forehead's line

The curved and curtal lip
Full in companionship
With that lip's overplus,
Proud and most sumptuous,

Which draws its curve within,
Swelling the faultless chin?
What artist knows the tech-
nique of the Doric neck:

The line that keeps with all
The features vertical,
Crowned with the thickly rolled
And corrugated gold?

The curious hands are lost
On the sweet Asian coast,
That made the coins enwrought
(Fairer than all they bought)

With emblems round the proud
Untroubled face of god
And goddess. Or they lie
At Syracuse hard by

The fountain in Arethuse.
Therefore from Syracuse
I send this face to her
Whose face is lovelier,

Alas, and as remote
As hers around whose throat
The curving fishes swim,
As round a fountain's brim.

It shows on the reverse
Pherenikos the horse;
And that's as it should be:
Horses she loves, for she

Is come of the old stock,
Lords of the limestone rock
And acres fit to breed
Many a likely steed,

Straight in the back and bone
With head high, like her own,
And blood that, tamed and mild,
Can suddenly go wild.

Oliver St. John Gogarty (1878–1957)

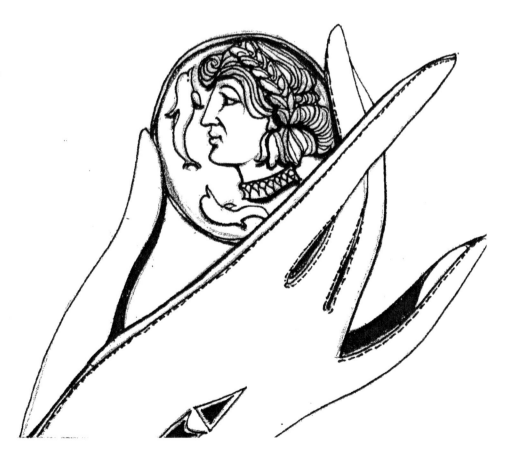

37

Lapis Lazuli (for Harry Clifton)

Two Chinamen, behind them a third,
Are carved in lapis lazuli,
Over them flies a long-legged bird,
A symbol of longevity;
The third, doubtless a serving-man,
Carries a musical instrument.

Every discolouration of the stone,
Every accidental crack or dent,
Seems a water-course or an avalanche,
Or lofty slope where it still snows
Though doubtless plum or cherry-branch
Sweetens the little half-way house
Those Chinamen climb towards, and I
Delight to imagine them seated there;
There, on the mountain and the sky,
On all the tragic scene they stare.
One asks for mournful melodies;
Accomplished fingers begin to play.
Their eyes mid many wrinkles, their eyes,
Their ancient, glittering eyes, are gay.

W. B. Yeats (1865–1939)

I have omitted the first twenty-four lines
of the poem, which are only by association
relevant to the theme of this book.

38

Roman De Rou (The Romance of Rollo, Robert I, Duke of Normandy)

[He]
Saw Constantine in Rome display'd
In manly shape, of copper made,
Of copper is the horse also,
No wind nor rain them overthrow.
Such is the fame and the honour
Of Constantine the Emperor.

[The Anglo-Norman poet] Robert Wace (1100–75)

39

L'envoi

Connoisseurs, that once as children played beside the summer sea,
Searching where the weed and shingle held in tangled mystery
Painted shell, and glittering pebble, to be garnered jealously –
Older, wiser eyes grown keener, hunting ever as of yore
In the narrow streets of cities, up and down thro' mart and store
On the outlook still for treasures lost upon Time's shifting shore.
Born, but never manufactured, Connoisseurs are much the same
Be it gem, or ware, or picture – care for neither mark nor name,
Note its beauty, stamp its value, ask no eulogy from fame;
To possess, their fixed intention, if? – but there, we must not tell
How collectors seek and cover, scheme to gain, and think it well
Just to hold, to keep, to treasure, barter, buy – but never sell.
'Things of beauty, Joys for ever' – if 'tis true what poets say,
Give the Connoisseur such welcome, that it cannot choose but stay.

L. Baily

This poem, by the mother of the first
Editor of *The Connoisseur* (J.T. Herbert
Baily, 1865-1914), appeared in the
first issue of the magazine, September, 1901.

40

At Auction

O Persian painter, how I grudge your dreams!
I too have flower-thoughts, harvested on ways
You would have gloried in, I too see gems
In the far heaven, some might even grave
Your-subtly woven dyes;
Thoughts blossoming at dawn, the fantasies
A child has when it rambles in the woods
For the first time, the moods
That lovers know whose hands unpurposed meet
As they stoop down to cull the meadow-sweet.

How different is your vision-world! To me
It's like a garden of old odorous herbs
Where white-smocked humming-bees drone lazily
In the long summer days, and naught disturbs
Them in their meandering tour
Of thyme and basil and prim lavender
Excepting haply certain footsteps come
As the grey twigs grow dumb,
To linger in the lane of rosemary
That far-off twilights gathered by the sea.

Such is the warp and woof you've made divine;
A scent; a slumber; an enchanted place;
Beyond it, hung with arabesque and vine,
Fabulous animals and scenes of chase;
Somehow you harmonize
Nature's antagonists; I half surmise
They mirror you, the world contemplative
In which you used to live,
And ringing round it, the fast foolish strife
Of lion and lynx and cloven hippogriff.

New conquerors from uncouth countries came
And passed you by; dust-bitten caravans
With strange apparelling of silk and gem,
With cinnamons and sapphires and sedans,
Came, halted, passed you by;
Some were for Venice, some for Tartary;
They sold, they sacked, they traded, tortured, gamed,
Grew rich, royal, mighty, famed,
While stitch by stitch the prunus left your hand
With none to see from Fez to Samarkand.

None only Allah; all your prunus trees,
Your bowers of citron, starry jessamine,
All were for Him who rives hypocrisies
And knows the hostel 'neath its gaudy sign.
Is it not He who made
The fig-tree where you sat in silvery shade?
Then let them cluster round His holy gates,
Ripe figs, rare pomegranates;
You've taken for device – 'One life, one gift,'
And Allah answers – 'Whoso gives, hath lived.'

Of other sort their trafficking to-day!
E'en now they're holding up their impious prize
Above the rostrum, and begin to bray
And brag as though possession made them wise.
By what themselves allege
They stand attaint in grossest sacrilege.
'A clever dealer brought it from the east.'
'He heard of it at feast
And bribed the keepers of the Holy Place.'
''Twas wasted where it was; 'twas hard to trace.'

And in a moment, when the bidding's done,
This jewel, where five centuries have prayed
And worshipped, this pure-flowered paragon
Of constancy where not a seed has strayed
On wings of the night air,
This, the epitome of all that's fair,
Ousting revenges, like wild animals,
To its remotest walls,
Will be a thing to boast of, a pretence
Of culture at the beck of insolence.

Or may it be the fragrance of the plum
That rounded to your touch is latent still
In those dark indigos, and certain dumb
Crude doubts will ask a hearing on the skill
Of its new factory-lord,
As he sets foot upon your crimson sward?
He makes ten hundreds such each working day;
There's not one strews the way
Of the white angel to and fro the soul;
He's no such wool-stuffs on his patent-roll.

What *was* the magic of those camel-tents
In the quiet desert, and the fruiting-trees?
To ply your craft you had no implements,
To learn it no soft seminars of ease,
Whiles he has had them both
And knows your labours for a kind of sloth.
Yet now his motto – 'We are self-contained,'
Is streaked with question, veined:
'The pulses beating in a million cogs
Are *almost* human,' say his catalogues.

James Elroy Flecker (1884–1915)

41

In a local Museum

They stood – rain pelting at window, shrouded sea –
Tenderly hand in hand, too happy to talk;
And there, its amorous eye intent on me,
Plautus impennis, the extinct Great Auk.

Walter de la Mare (1873–1956)

42

Housman at Sotheby's

On 9 July 1968, a large collection of the papers of Laurence Housman was sold at Sotheby's in London. It included an unpublished poem by his brother, A.E. Housman, and three unpublished autograph letters from Oscar Wilde to Laurence Housman. The editor of this book, who at that time was sale room correspondent of *The Times*, began his report on the sale with a parody of Housman's verse. This is believed to be the first time a *Times* news report was couched in verse.

> At Sotheby's the hammer raps
> Like drum-taps for a slaughtered lad
> And autographs are sold to chaps
> With half the heart their authors had.
>
> O never fear the poet's curse:
> His corpse must rot, his soul may burn:
> Like him, the copies of his verse
> Are sold 'not subject to return'.

Bevis Hillier (1940–)

43

A Bellarmine Jug

It was at one time thought that Bellarmine jugs were so named because the beard mask on their necks was intended as a caricature of Cardinal Bellarmine (1542-1621), the idea being that he was cordially detested in the Protestant German and low countries where many such stoneware jugs were made. This theory has been satisfactorily demolished: an example exists dated 1550, when the future Cardinal was only eight years old – so, as Anthony Thwaite has said in a definitive article (*The Connoisseur*, April 1973), 'clearly the name was a *post hoc* jest'. The earliest literary reference to bellarmines is in Bulwer's *Artificial Changeling* (1563), in which it is said of a formal doctor that:

> the fashion of his beard was just, for all the world,
> like those upon Flemish jugs, bearing in gross the form of
> a broom, narrow above and broad beneath.

Ben Jonson also mentioned them in 1613 (in the masque *The Gypsies Metamorphos'd*) and 1614 (in *Bartholomew Fair*). But the first time the word 'bellarmine' is applied to the jug is in the following extract from William Cartwright's play *The Ordinary*, of 1634.

> Thou Thing,

Thy belly looks like to some strutting hill
O'ershadowed with thy rough beard like a wood;
Or like a larger jug, that some men call
A bellarmine, but we a Conscience;
Whereon the lewder hand of pagan workmen
Over the proud, ambitious head hath carved
An idol large with beard episcopal,
Making the vessel look like tyrant Eglon.
William Cartwright (1611–43)

44

Ode on a Grecian Urn

Thou still unravish'd bride of quietness,
Thou foster-child of silence and slow time,
Sylvan historian, who canst thus express
A flow'ry tale more sweetly than our rhyme:
What leaf-fring'd legend haunts about thy shape
Of deities or mortals, or of both.
In Temple or the dales of Arcady?
What men or gods are these? What maidens loth?
What mad pursuit? What struggle to escape?
What pipes and timbrels? What wild ecstasy?

Heard melodies are sweet, but those unheard
Are sweeter: therefore, ye soft pipes, play on;
Not to the sensual ear, but, more endear'd,
Pipe to the spirit ditties of no tone:
Fair youth, beneath the trees, thou canst not leave
Thy song, nor ever can those trees be bare;
Bold Lover, never, never canst thou kiss,
Though winning near the goal – yet, do not grieve;.
She cannot fade, though thou hast not thy bliss,
For ever wilt thou love, and she be fair!

Ah, happy happy boughs! that cannot shed
Your leaves, nor ever bid the Spring adieu;
And, happy melodist, unwearied,
For ever piping songs for ever new;
More happy love! more happy, happy love!
For ever warm and still to be enjoy'd,
For ever panting, and for ever young;
All breathing human passion far above,
That leaves a heart high-sorrowful and cloy'd,
A burning forehead, and a parching tongue.

Who are these coming to the sacrifice?
To what green altar, O mysterious priest,
Lead'st thou that heifer lowing at the skies,
And all her silken flanks with garlands drest?
What little town by river or sea shore,

Or mountain-built with peaceful citadel,
Is emptied of this folk, this pious morn?
And, little town, thy streets for evermore
Will silent be; and not a soul to tell
Why thou art desolate, can e'er return.

O Attic shape! Fair attitude! with brede
Of marble men and maidens overwrought,
With forest branches and the trodden weed;
Thou silent form, dost tease us out of thought
As doth eternity: Cold Pastoral!
When old age shall this generation waste,
Thou shalt remain, in midst of other woe
Than ours, a friend to man, to whom thou say'st,
'Beauty is truth, truth Beauty,' – that is all
Ye know on earth, and all ye need to know.

John Keats (1795–1821)

45

Mona Lisa

(W.B. Yeats, in *The Oxford Book of Modern Verse*, 1936, broke down Walter Pater's famous 'prose' passage on Leonardo's *Mona Lisa* into the following blank verse lines.)

She is older than the rocks among which she sits;
Like the Vampire,
She has been dead many times,
And learned the secrets of the grave;
And has been a diver in deep seas,
And keeps their fallen day about her;
And trafficked for strange webs with Eastern merchants;
And, as Leda,
Was the mother of Helen of Troy,
And, as St. Anne,
Was the mother of Mary;
And all this has been to her but as the sound of lyres and flutes,
And lives
Only in the delicacy
With which it has moulded the changing lineaments,
And tinged the eyelids and the hands.

Walter Pater (1839–94)

46

The Fair Brass

An effigy of brass
Trodden by careless feet
Of worshippers that pass,
Beautiful and complete,

Lieth in the sombre aisle
Of this old church unwreckt,
And still from modern style
Shielded by kind neglect.

It shows a warrior arm'd:
Across his iron breast
His hands by death are charm'd
To leave his sword at rest,

Wherewith he led his men
O'ersea, and smote to hell
The astonisht Saracen,
Nor doubted he did well.

Would we could teach our sons
His trust in face of doom,
Or give our bravest ones
A comparable tomb:

Such as to look on shrives
The heart of half its care;
So in each line survives
The spirit that made it fair;

So fair the characters,
With which the dusty scroll,
That tells his title, stirs
A requiem for his soul.

Robert Bridges (1844–1930)

I have omitted the last four stanzas, which are in main a tirade against modern war memorials, which 'In mournful marbles gilt,/ Deface the beauteous walls/ By growing glory built.' Others must have shared Bridges' views: in Merstham Church, Surrey, there is a memorial brass, in the antique style, showing a soldier in puttees who died in the Great War.

47

The Willow Pattern Rhyme

Two pigeons flying high,
Chinese vessels sailing by:
Weeping willows hanging o'er,
Bridge with three men, if not four:
Chinese temples, there they stand,
Seem to take up all the land:
Apple trees with apples on,
A pretty fence to end my song.

Anon.

48

The 'Mary Gloster' (1894)

(The dying captain addresses his son, educated at 'Harrer an' Trinity College'.)

The things I knew was proper you wouldn't thank me to give,
And the things I knew was rotten you said was the way to live.
For you muddled with books and pictures, an' china an' etchin's an' fans,
And your rooms at college was beastly – more like a whore's than a man's.

Rudyard Kipling (1865—1936)

49

Ballade of the Book-hunter

In torrid heats of late July,
In March, beneath the bitter *bise*,
He book-hunts while the loungers fly, –
He book-hunts, though December freeze;
In breeches baggy at the knees,
And heedless of the public jeers,
For these, for these, he hoards his fees, –
Aldines, Bodonis, Elzevirs.

No dismal stall escapes his eye,
He turns o'er tomes of low degrees,
There soiled romanticists may lie,
Or Restoration comedies;
Each tract that flutters in the breeze
For him is charged with hopes and fears,
In mouldy novels fancy sees
Aldines, Bodonis, Elzevirs.

With restless eyes that peer and spy,
Sad eyes that heed not skies nor trees,
In dismal nooks he loves to pry,
Whose motto evermore is *Spes*!
But ah! the fabled treasure flees;
Grown rarer with the fleeting years,
In rich men's shelves they take their ease, –
Aldines, Bodonis, Elsevirs!

ENVOY
Prince, all the things that tease and please, –
Fame, hope, wealth, kisses, cheers, and tears,
What are they but such toys as these –
Aldines, Bodonis, Elzevirs?

Andrew Lang (1844–1912)

50

Ode on a Mid-Victorian Centre Ornament

Oh thou maid of buxom beauty!
    Lifting up to hold the cake,
An impossible creation,
    Which is surely a mistake.
I have often wept in thinking
    How terribly your arms must ache.

Oh thou fish in beauty trailing
    At each corner, are you dead?
If you are not I will warn you
    'Lie the other way instead:
Staying long in that position
    Makes the blood run to your head.'

Oh you thousand strange devices,
    Can you tell me what you mean
By trailing creepy curly tendrils
    Over every varied scene,
Infringing on the neat inscription
    'A presentation to the Dean...'?

John Betjeman (1906–84)

51

To an Unknown Bust in the British Museum
'Sermons in Stones'

Who were you once? Could we but guess,
We might perchance more boldly
Define the patient weariness
That sets your lips so coldly;
You 'lived', we know, for blame and fame;
But sure, to friend or foeman,
You bore some more distinctive name
Than mere 'B.C.', – and 'Roman'?

Your pedestal should help us much.
Thereon your acts, your title,
(Secure from cold Oblivion's touch!)
Had doubtless due recital;
Vain hope! – not even deeds can last!
That stone, of which you're *minus*,
Maybe with all your virtues past
Endows ... a TIGERLINUS!

We seek it not; we should not find.
But still, it needs no magic
To tell you wore, like most mankind,
Your comic mask and tragic;
And held that things were false and true,
Felt angry or forgiving,
As step by step you stumbled through
This life-long task ... of living!

You tried the *cul-de-sac* of Thought;
The *montagne Russe* of Pleasure;
You found the best Ambition brought
Was strangely short of measure;
You watched, at last, the fleet days fly,
Till – drowsier and colder –
You felt MERCURIUS loitering by
To touch you on the shoulder.

'Twas then (why not?) the whim would come
That howso Time should garble
Those deeds of yours when you were dumb,
At least you'd live – in Marble;
You smiled to think that after days,
At least, in Bust or Statue,
(We all have sick-bed dreams!) would gaze,
Not quite incurious, at you.

We gaze; *we* pity you, be sure!
In truth, Death's worst inaction
Must be less tedious to endure
Than nameless petrifaction;
Far better, in some nook unknown,
To sleep for once – and soundly –
Than still survive in wistful stone,
Forgotten more profoundly!

Austin Dobson (1840–1921)

52

Upon the Sight of a Beautiful Picture

Painted by Sir G.H. Beaumont, Bart. [composed August, 1811 – Published 1815.]

> Praised be the Art whose subtle power could stay
> Yon cloud, and fix it in that glorious shape;
> Nor would permit the thin smoke to escape,
> Nor those bright sunbeams to forsake the day;
> Which stopped that band of travellers on their way,
> Ere they were lost within the shady wood;
> And showed the Bark upon the glassy flood
> For ever anchored in her sheltering bay.
> Soul-soothing Art! whom Morning, Noontide, Even,
> Do serve with all their changeful pageantry;
> Thou, with ambition modest yet sublime,
> Here, for the sight of mortal man, hast given
> To one brief moment caught from fleeting time
> The appropriate calm of blest eternity.

William Wordsworth (1770–1850)

53

Peter Paul Rubens at Het Steen, Ca. 1636

In a *draught* or *designe*, the Artist must *fancie* every circumstance of his matter in hand; as usually Rubens would (with his Arms a cross) sit musing upon his work for some time; and in an instant the in livelinesse of spirit, with a nimble hand would force out his over-charged *brain* into description as not to be contained in the Compass of ordinary practice, but by a violent driving on of passion. The *Commotions* of the mind, are not to be cooled by slow performance: discreet diligence, brings forth *Excellence*: *Care*, and *Exercise*, are the chiefest precepts of art. (Sir William Sanderson, *Graphice*, London 1658).

In his time he has walked with kings
and painted the rascals, too,
lofted to God on eagle-wings,
(all seen *di sotto in sù*).

But he doesn't find that ridiculous,
being *croyant* as they come;
expeditious yet meticulous,
this master of tit and bum.

Yes, reliable and circumspect,
he meets deadlines and makes money,
but there's something about him you'd never expect,
like the bitter taste in honey;

else why, when he's down on his country estate
with a young and peach-skinned wife,
doesn't he doze in the morning late,
in the evening of his life?

No, he climbs his tower to read the sky,
to watch what moves on the plain
and to stare the rising sun in the eye
where he's Lord of the Manor at Steen.

In his room he bides, arms crossed, quite still
before flick of brush or scumble;
for the mind's commotions mustn't chill
while fingers fumble.

Like the harvesters who stack his straw,
like the peasants in the wain,
like his cowman – I'm more than a little in awe
of the Master of Het Steen.

John Mallet (1930-)

54

The Punch Bowl

This ancient silver bowl of mine, – it tells of good old times,
Of joyous days, and jolly nights, and merry Christmas chimes;
They were a free and jovial race, but honest, brave and true,
That dipped their ladle in the punch when this old bowl was new.

A Spanish galleon brought the bar, – so runs the ancient tale;
'Twas hammered by an Antwerp smith, whose arm was like a flail;
And now and then between the strokes, for fear his strength should fail
He wiped his brow, and quaffed a cup of good old Flemish ale.

'Twas purchased by an English squire to please his loving dame,
Who saw the cherubs, and conceived a longing for the same;
And oft, as on the ancient stock another twig was found,
'Twas filled with caudle spiced and hot, and handed smoking round.

But, changing hands, it reached at length a Puritan divine,
Who used to follow Timothy, and take a little wine,
But hated punch and prelacy; and so it was, perhaps,
He went to Leyden, where he found conventicles and schnaps.

And then, of course you know what's next, – it left the Dutchman's shore
With those that in the *Mayflower* came – a hundred souls and more –
Along with all the furniture to fill their new abodes –
To judge by what is still on hand, at least a hundred loads.

'Twas on a dreary winter's eve, the night was closing dim,
When old Miles Standish took the bowl, and filled it to the brim;
The little captain stood and stirred the posset with his sword,
And all his sturdy men-at-arms were ranged about the board.

He poured the fiery Hollands in – the man that never feared,
He took a long and solemn draught, and wiped his yellow beard;
And one by one the musketeers – the men that fought and prayed –
All drank as 'twere their mother's milk, and not a man afraid.

That night, affrighted from his nest, the screaming eagle flew,
He heard the Pequot's ringing whoop, the soldiers' wild halloo;
And there the sachem learned the rule he taught to kith and kin,
'Run from the white man when you find he smells of Hollands gin!'

A hundred years, and fifty more, had spread their leaves and snows,
A thousand rubs had flattened down each little cherub's nose;
When once again the bowl was filled, but not in mirth or joy,
'Twas mingled by a mother's hand to cheer her parting boy.

'Drink, John,' she said, "twill do you good – poor child, you'll never bear
This working in the dismal trench, out in the midnight air;
And if – God bless me – you were hurt, 'twould keep away the chill:'
So John did drink – and well he wrought that night at Bunker's Hill.

I tell you there was generous warmth in good old English cheer;
I tell you 'twas a pleasant thought to bring its symbol here.
'Tis but the fool that loves excess; hast thou a drunken soul?
Thy bane is in thy shallow skull, not in my silver bowl!

I love the memory of the past – its pressed yet fragrant flowers –
The moss that clothes its broken walls – the ivy on its towers
Nay, this poor bauble is bequeathed – my eyes grow moist and dim,
To think of all the vanished joys that danced around its brim.

Then fill a fair and honest cup, and bear it straight to me;
The goblet hallows all it holds, whate'er the liquid be;
And may the cherubs on its face protect me from the sin,
That dooms one to those dreadful words – 'My dear, where *have* you been?'

Oliver Wendell Holmes (1809–94)

55

Prologue to 'Proverbs in Porcelain'

Assume that we are friends. Assume
A common taste for old costume, –
Old pictures, – books. Then dream us sitting –
Us two – in some soft-lighted room.

Outside, the wind; – the 'ways are mire.'
We, with our faces toward the fire,
Finish the feast not full but fitting,
Watch the light-leaping flames aspire.

Silent at first, in time we glow;
Discuss 'eclectics', high and low;
Inspect engravings, 'twixt us passing
The fancies of DETROY, MOREAU.

'Reveils' and 'Couchers', 'Balls' and 'Fêtes';
Anon we glide to 'crocks' and plates,
Grow eloquent on glaze and classing,
And half-pathetic over 'states'

Then I produce my Prize, in truth; –
Six groups in SEVRES, fresh as Youth,
And rare as Love. You pause, you wonder
(Pretend to doubt the marks, forsooth!)

And so we fall to why and how
The fragile figures smile and bow;
Divine, at length, the fable under...
Thus grew the 'Scenes' that follow now.

Austin Dobson (1840–1921)

56

Old Yearsley Song

In Yearsley there are pancheons made,
By Willie Wedgwood, that young blade.

ANON.

It is not known whether Willie Wedgwood was an ancestor or kinsman of the great Josiah Wedgwood, but it seems likely that he was.

The site of the Wedgwood pottery was first discovered when clay was being dug for the tilery on Sir George Wombwell's estate, Yearsley, Yorkshire, in the middle of the nineteenth century.

The first mention of Wedgwood in the Yearsley area is in the Coxwold parish register of 1653 when, on November 8, John Wedgwood and Elizabeth Harrison were married.

From the mid-seventeenth century until his death in 1682, John Wedgwood and his son John (who died in 1707) made large cisterns, 'puzzle jugs', plates and bowls at Yearsley. In the Glaisher Collection at Cambridge there is a puzzle jug inscribed 'John Wedg Wood 1692'. A cistern at Ampleforth Abbey is scratched 'John Wedg Wood'.

After John's death the pottery was continued by William, his son. He produced large bowls or pancheons. In the Glaisher collection is a brown-glazed cistern ascribed to him, bearing the initials 'WW'.

57

A Psalm of Montreal

The city of Montreal is one of the most rising and, in many respects, most agreeable on the American continent, but its inhabitants are as yet too busy with commerce to care greatly about the masterpieces of old Greek Art. In the Montreal Museum of Natural History I came upon two plaster casts, one of the Antinous and the other of the Discobolus – not the good one, but in my poem, of course, I intend the good one – banished from public view to a room where were all manner of skins, plants, snakes, insects, etc., and, in the middle of these, an old man stuffing an owl.

'Ah,' said I, 'so you have some antiques here; why don't you put them where people can see them?'

'Well, sir,' answered the custodian, 'you see they are rather vulgar.' He then talked a great deal and said his brother did all Mr. Spurgeon's printing.

The dialogue – perhaps true, perhaps imaginary, perhaps a little of the one and a little of the other – between the writer and this old man gave rise to the lines that follow:

> Stowed away in a Montreal lumber room
> The Discobolus standeth and turneth his face to the wall;
> Dusty, cobweb-covered, maimed, and set at naught,
> Beauty crieth in an attic and no man regardeth:
> O God! O Montreal!
>
> Beautiful by night and day, beautiful in summer and winter,
> Whole or maimed, always and alike beautiful –
> He preacheth gospel of grace to the skins of owls
> And to one who seasoneth the skins of Canadian owls:
> O God! O Montreal!
>
> When I saw him I was wroth and I said, 'O Discobolus!
> Beautiful Discobolus, a Prince both among gods and men!
> What doest thou here, how camest thou hither, Discobolus,
> Preaching gospel in vain to the skins of owls?'
> O God! O Montreal!
>
> And I turned to the man of skins and said unto him, 'O thou man of skins,
> Wherefore hast thou done thus to shame the beauty of the Discobolus?'
> But the Lord had hardened the heart of the man of skins
> And he answered, 'My brother-in-law is haberdasher to Mr. Spurgeon.'
> O God! O Montreal!

'The Discobulus is put here because he is vulgar,
He has neither vest not pants with which to cover his limbs;
I, Sir, am a person of most respectable connections –
My brother-in-law is haberdasher to Mr. Spurgeon.'
O God! O Montreal!

Then I said, 'O brother-in-law to Mr. Spurgeon's haberdasher,
Who seasonest also the skins of Canadian owls,
Thou callest trousers "pants," whereas I call them "trousers,"
Therefore thou art in hell-fire and may the Lord pity thee!'
O God! O Montreal!

'Preferrest thou the gospel of Montreal to the gospel of Hellas,
The gospel of thy connection with Mr. Spurgeon's haberdashery to
the gospel of the Discobolus?'
Yet none the less blasphemed he beauty saying, 'The Discobolus
hath no gospel,
But my brother-in-law is haberdasher to Mr. Spurgeon.'
O God! O Montreal!

Samuel Butler (1835–1902)

58

Address to the Mummy in Belzoni's Exhibition (1819)

And thou hast walked about (how strange a story!)
In Thebes's streets three thousand years ago,
When the Memnonium was in all its glory,
And time had not begun to overthrow
Those temples, palaces, and piles stupendous,
Of which the very ruins are tremendous.

Speak! for thou long enough hast acted dummy;
Thou hast a tongue, come let us hear its tune;
Thou'rt standing on thy legs, above ground, Mummy,
Revisiting the glimpses of the moon,
Not like thin ghosts, or disembodied creatures,
But with thy bones and flesh, and limbs and features.

Tell us, for doubtless thou canst recollect,
To whom should we assign the Sphinx's fame?
Was Cheops or Cephrenes architect
Of either pyramid that bears his name?
Is Pompey's pillar really a misnomer?
Had Thebes a hundred gates, as sung by Homer?

Perhaps thou wert a mason, and forbidden
By oath to tell the mysteries of thy trade,
Then say what secret melody was hidden
In Memnon's statue, which at sunrise played?
Perhaps thou wert a priest – if so, my struggles
Are vain, for priestcraft never owns its juggles.

Perchance that very hand, now pinioned flat,
Has hob-a-nobbed with Pharaoh, glass to glass;
Or dropped a halfpenny in Homer's hat,
Or doffed thine own to let Queen Dido pass:
Or held, by Solomon's own invitation,
A torch at the great Temple's dedication.

I need not ask thee if that hand, when armed,
Has any Roman soldier mauled and knuckled,
For thou wert dead, and buried, and embalmed,
Ere Romulus and Remus had been suckled;
Antiquity appears to have begun
Long after thy primeval race was run.

Thou couldst develop, if that withered tongue
Might tell us what those sightless orbs have seen,
How the world looked when it was fresh and young,
And the great deluge still had left it green;
Or was it then so old, that history's pages
Contained no record of its early ages?

Didst thou not hear the pother o'er thy head,
When the great Persian conqueror, Cambyses,
Marched armies o'er thy tomb with thundering tread,
O'erthrew Osiris, Orus, Apis, Isis?
And shook the pyramids with fear and wonder,

When the gigantic Memnon fell asunder?
If the tomb's secrets may not be confessed,
The nature of thy private life unfold;
A heart has throbbed beneath that leathern breast,
And tears adown that dusky cheek have rolled.
Have children climbed those knees, and kissed that face?
What was thy name and station, age, and race?

Statue of flesh, immortal of the dead!
Imperishable type of evanescence,
Posthumous man, who quitt'st thy narrow bed
And standest undecayed within our presence –
Thou wilt hear nothing till the judgment morning,
Then the great trump shall thrill thee with its warning.

Why should this worthless tegument endure,
If its undying guest be lost for ever?
Oh! let us keep the soul embalmed and pure
In living virtue, that, when both must sever,
Although corruption may our frame consume,
The immortal spirit in the skies may bloom!

Horace Smith (1779–1849)

Smith wrote these lines after he had seen a mummy in Belzoni's exhibition in the Egyptian Hall, Piccadilly, in 1819. Belzoni had come to England from Padua in 1803, and after a short career as a showman, during which he posed as 'The Patagonian Samson' and as 'Grand Sultan of all the Conjurers', he became an explorer and excavator in Egypt, sending many valuable monuments, busts and sarcophagi to England.

59

For Antoine Watteau (1684–1721)

It has recently been suggested that the painting of 1717 by the French master Jeran-Antoine Watteau that has always been known as *The Embarkation for Cythera* actually shows people *leaving* the island of Cythera.

They neither come nor go at Cythera,
men and young women, moving in a trance,
their slippers glide in dance;
a noonday blackness beckons under boughs
in shadowed, sunken glades.
The Isle exhales its resin from dark fronds.

But here the painter coughs, knowing too well
tuberculosis drowns a man on land,
that to a sadder strand
the Ferryman must oar him early home.

I stand beside the easel, hold my breath
and will his brush to dip from knoll to knoll
to make the picture whole
with heads that turn and hopes that are betrayed,
as dusk encroaches and the satins fade.

John Mallet (1930-)

60

Ballade of Blue China

There's a joy without canker or cark,
There's a pleasure eternally new,
'Tis to gloat on the glaze and the mark
Of china that's ancient and blue;
Unchipp'd all the centuries through
It has pass'd, since the chime of it rang,
And they fashion'd it, figure and hue,
In the reign of the Emperor Hwang.

These dragons (their tails, you remark,
Into bunches of gillyflowers grew), –
When Noah came out of the ark,
Did these lie in wait for his crew?
They snorted, they snapp'd, and they slew,
They were mighty of fin and of fang,
And their portraits Celestials drew
In the reign of the Emperor Hwang.

Here's a pot with a cot in a park,
In a park where the peach-blossoms blew,
Where the lovers eloped in the dark,
Lived, died, and were changed into two
Bright birds that eternally flew
Through the boughs of the may, as they sang;
'Tis a tale was undoubtedly true
In the reign of the Emperor Hwang.

ENVOY

Come, snarl at my ecstasies, do,
Kind critic, your 'tongue has a tang'
But – a sage never heeded a shrew
In the reign of the Emperor Hwang.

Andrew Lang (1844–1912)

CREW ONLY

61

My Last Duchess

That's my last Duchess painted on the wall,
Looking as if she were alive. I call
That piece a wonder, now: Fra Pandolf's hands
Worked busily a day, and there she stands.
Will't please you sit and look at her? I said
'Fra Pandolf' by design, for never read
Strangers like you that pictured countenance,
The depth and passion of its earnest glance,
But to myself they turned (since none puts by
The curtain I have drawn for you, but I)
And seemed as they would ask me, if they durst,
How such a glance came there; so, not the first
Are you to turn and ask thus. Sir, 'twas not
Her husband's presence only, called that spot
Of joy into the Duchess's cheek: perhaps
Fra Pandolf chanced to say 'Her mantle laps
'Over my lady's wrist too much,' or 'Paint
'Must never hope to reproduce the faint
'Half-flush that dies along her throat:'
such stuff
Was courtesy, she thought, and cause enough
For calling up that spot of joy. She had
A heart – how shall I say? – too soon made glad,
Too easily impressed; she liked whate'er
She looked on, and her looks went everywhere.
Sir, 'twas all one! My favour at her breast,
The dropping of the daylight in the West,
The bough of cherries some officious fool
Broke in the orchard for her, the white mule
She rode with round the terrace – all and each
Would draw from her alike the approving speech,
Or blush, at least. She thanked men, – good!
but thanked
Somehow – I know not how – as if she ranked
My gift of a nine-hundred-years-old name
With anybody's gift. Who'd stoop to blame
This sort of trifling? Even had you skill
In speech – (which I have not) – to make your will

Quite clear to such an one, and say, 'Just this
'Or that in you disgust me; here you miss,
'Or there exceed the mark' – and if she let
Herself be lessoned so, nor plainly set
Her wits to yours, forsooth, and made excuse,
– E'en then would be some stooping; and I choose
Never to stoop. Oh sir, she smiled, no doubt,
Whene'er I passed her; but who passed without
Much the same smile? This grew; I gave commands;
Then all smiles stopped together. There she stands
As if alive. Will't please you rise? We'll meet
The company below, then. I repeat,
The Count your master's known munificence
Is ample warrant that no just pretence
Of mine for dowry will be disallowed;
Though his fair daughter's self, as I avowed
At starting, is my object. Nay, we'll go
Together down, sir. Notice Neptune, though
Taming a sea-horse, thought a rarity,
Which Claus of Innsbruck cast in bronze for me!

Robert Browning (1812–89)

62

The Old Arm-chair

I love it, I love it; and who shall dare
To chide me for loving that old Arm-chair?
I've treasured it long as a sainted prize;
I've bedewed it with tears, and embalmed it with sighs.
'Tis bound by a thousand bands to my heart;
Not a tie will break, not a link will start.
Would ye learn the spell? – a mother sat there;
And a sacred thing is that old Arm-chair.

In Childhood's hour I lingered near
The hallowed seat with listening ear;
And gentle words that mother would give;
To fit me to die, and teach me to live.
She told me shame would never betide,
With truth for my creed and God for my guide;
She taught me to lisp my earliest prayer;
As I knelt beside that old Arm-chair.

I sat and watched her many a day,
When her eye grew dim, and her locks were grey:
And I almost worshipped her when she smiled,
And turned from her Bible, to bless her child.
Years rolled on; but the last one sped –
My idol was shattered; my earth-star fled:
I learnt how much the heart can bear,
When I saw her die in that old Arm-chair.

'Tis past, 'tis past, but I gaze on it now
With quivering breath and throbbing brow:
'Twas there she nursed me; 'twas there she died:
And Memory flows with lava tide.
Say it is folly, and deem me weak,
While the scalding drops start down my cheek;
But I love it, I love it; and cannot tear
My soul from a mother's old Arm-chair.

Eliza Cook (1818–89)

63

The Cane-bottomed Chair

In tattered old slippers that toast at the bars,
And a ragged old jacket perfumed with cigars,
Away from the world and its toils and its cares,
I've a snug little kingdom up four pair of stairs.

This snug little chamber is crammed in all nooks
With worthless old knicknacks and silly old books,
And foolish old odds, and foolish old ends,
Cracked bargains from brokers, cheap keepsakes from friends.

Old armour, prints, pictures, pipes, china (all cracked);
Old rickety tables, and chairs broken-backed;
A twopenny treasury, worthless to see;
What matter? 'tis pleasant to you, friend, and me.

That praying-rug came from a Turcoman's camp;
By Tiber once twinkled that brazen old lamp;
A Mameluke fierce yonder dagger has drawn:
'Tis a murderous knife to toast muffins upon.

Long, long through the hours and the night and the chimes
Here we talk of old books and old friends and old times;
As we sit in a fog made of rich Latakie
This chamber is pleasant to you, friend, and me.

But of all the cheap treasures that garnish my nest,
There's one that I love and I cherish the best;
For the finest of couches that's padded with hair
I never would change thee, my cane-bottomed chair.

'Tis a bandy-legged, high-shouldered, worm-eaten seat,
With a creaking old back and twisted old feet;
But since the fair morning when Fanny sat there
I bless thee and love thee, old cane-bottomed chair.

It was but a moment she sat in this place,
She'd a scarf on her neck, and a smile on her face,
A smile on her face and a rose in her hair,
And she sat there and bloomed in my cane-bottomed chair.

And so I have valued my chair ever since
Like the shrine of a saint, or the throne of a prince;
Saint Fanny my patroness sweet I declare,
The queen of my heart and my cane-bottomed chair.

William Makepeace Thackeray (1811–63)

64

The Horn of Ulphus

The horn of Ulphus, a Saxon chief, is still preserved in the sacristy of York Minster. It is of immense size, and is probably the tip of an elephant's tusk. It is curiously carved, and has become from age, a rich mellow colour. Ulphus is said to have filled it full of wine when he presented his lands, kneeling at the high altar, and as he rose drained it at a draught to the honour of St. Peter. We have, by a fair poetical licence, supposed it to have been used at civic banquets by the monarchs who have at various times visited the northern capital. The Horn, we may add, is undoubtedly of Eastern origin; and, if not brought from Antioch by some Roman proconsul, may have been part of a crusader's spoil at Acre or Damietta – York Cathedral is dedicated to St. Peter.

Bearded kings have drained thee oft,
'Mid the reapers in the croft:
Salves have frothed thee for the Caesar,
Watching in the glebe the leaser.

Round the torch-lit raven banner,
Waiting like the Jews for manna,
Sat the Danes, and mixèd up
Hubba's blood in Ulpha's cup.

Vowing, by their sable raven,
They would slay the Saxon craven,
And the hare should crouch and breed,
Where the Seven Princes feed.

Next the mailèd Norman came,
Fast before him burnt the flame,
Pestilence his herald fleet,
Famine shivering at his feet.

Where his charger's red feet trod,
Barren grew the blighted sod,
All before him sweet and fair,
All behind him scorch and bare.

Brimming full the swart crusader,
Pledged in thee the turbaned trader,
When he sheathed his broken brand,
By Damascus' burning sand.

When the proud Plantagenet
With the Dame of Cyprus met,
He before the Virgin's shrine,
Filled thee full of Gascon wine.

Grimly swore by lady's love,
By her mantle, brooch, and glove,
For her sake he'd snap a lance
In the very heart of France.

Scarce a year had passed away,
John came scowling from the fray,
Prodigals and jesters all,
Held at York their festival.

Portly abbot all askance,
Trembled at his wily glance,
When he saw the altar plate
Glitter through the cloister grate.

Wounded Stephen sorely spent
With the jostling tournament,
Swearing 'twas a kingly cup,
Bade his jester take a sup.

Edward, travel-worn and hot,
From his foray on the Scot,
Cried for wine his thirst to stanch,
'Wallace, Wallace! *ma revanche.*'

Faint and pale the wounded king[8]
Dipped thee in St. Peter's spring,
As through aisle and chapel dim,
Came the pealing battle hymn.

Henry, fresh from Agincourt,
Held thee up aloft in sport,
Bade an archer at a gulp,
Drain thee without aid or help.

She of Anjou, full of scorn,
Raised unto her lips this horn,
As she leapt upon her barb,
All a man but for the garb.

Sleepless Richard called for thee,
Cursing the sweet Litany,
As it rose like a perfume,
From St. Peter's holy tomb.

Henry swore to courtier pliant,
Thou wert goblet for a giant;
Poured the last drop on the stones,
Vowing by A'Becket's bones,

Not a lord in all his train,
Such a cup as that could drain;
Then he shouted for the chalice,
From the shrine of good St. Alice.

Rowley and his clustering, fair,
Perfumes tossing from their hair,
Laughed as with a pouting lip;
Every beauty took a sip.

George W. Thornbury (1828–76)

<hr>

8 The King of Scotland taken prisoner by Queen Philippa.

65

Dutch Portraits

To find myself in tears is a surprise –
Paintings don't often get to me like this:
These faces with their vulnerable eyes
And lips so soft that they invite a kiss;
The long-haired husband, gazing at his bride
With evident desire, his hand around
Her wrist, six years before she died –
Both so alive and so long underground.
And here's a husband who resembles you
When you were plump and bearded. It's too much.
He looks so happy and his wife does too,
Still smiling, now they can no longer touch.
Someone will read our story, by and by.
Perhaps they'll feel like this. Perhaps they'll cry.

Wendy Cope (1945–)

66

The China-mender

Good morning, Mr. What-d'ye-call! Well! here's another pretty job!
Lord help my Lady! – what a smash! – if you had only heard her sob!
It was all through Mr. Lambert: but for certain he was winy,
To think for to go to sit down on a table full of Chiny.
'Deuce take your stupid head!' says my Lady to his very face;
But politeness, you know, is nothing, when there's Chiny in the case:
And if ever a woman was fond of Chiny to a passion
It's my mistress, and all sorts of it, whether new or old fashion.
Her brother's a sea-captain, and brings her home ship loads –
Such bonzes, and such dragons, and nasty, squatting things like toads;
And great ninnoddin mandarins, with palsies in the head:
I declare I've often dreamt of them, and had nightmares in my bed.
But the frightfuller they are – lawk! she loves them all the better:
She'd have Old Nick himself made of Chiny if they'd let her.
Lawk-a-mercy! break her Chiny, and it's breaking her very heart;
If I touch'd it, she would very soon say, 'Mary, we must part.'
To be sure she *is* unlucky: only Friday comes Master Randall,
And breaks a broken spout, and fresh chips a tea-cup handle:
He's a dear, sweet little child, but he will so finger and touch,
And that's why my Lady doesn't take to children much.
Well! there's stupid Mr. Lambert, with his two great coat flaps,
Must go and sit down on the Dresden shepherdesses' laps,
As if there was no such things as rosewood chairs in the room;
I couldn't have made a greater sweep with the handle of the broom.
Mercy on us! how my mistress began to rave and tear!
Well! after all, there's nothing like good ironstone ware for wear.
If ever I marry, that's flat, I'm sure it won't be John Dockery,
I should be a wretched woman in a shop full of crockery.
I should never like to wipe it, though I love to be neat and tidy,
And afraid of mad bulls on market-days every Monday and Friday.
I'm very much mistook if Mr. Lambert's will be a catch;
The breaking the Chiny will be the breaking off of his own match.
Missis wouldn't have an angel, if he was careless about Chiny;
She never forgives a chip, if it's ever so small and tiny.
Lawk! I never saw a man in all my life in such a taking;
I could find in my heart to pity him for all his mischief-making.
To see him stand a-hammering and stammering, like a zany;
But what signifies apologies, if they wont mend old Chaney!

If he sent her up whole crates full, from Wedgwood's and Mr. Spode's,
He couldn't make amends for the crack'd mandarins and smash'd toads.
Well! every one has their tastes, but, for my part, my own self
I'd rather have the figures on my poor dear grandmother's old shelf:
A nice pea-green poll-parrot, and two reapers with brown ears of corns,
And a shepherd with a crook after a lamb with two gilt horns,
And such a Jemmy Jessamy in top-boots and sky-blue vest,
And a frill and flowered waistcoat, with a fine bowpot at the breast.
God help her, poor old soul! I shall come into 'em at her death,
Though she's a hearty woman for her years, except her shortness of breath.
Well! you think the things will mend – if they won't, Lord mend us all!
My Lady will go in fits, and Mr. Lambert won't need to call:
I'll be bound in any money, if I had a guinea to give,
He won't sit down again on Chiny the longest day he has to live.
Poor soul! I only hope it won't forbid his banns of marriage,
Or he'd better have sat behind on the spikes of my Lady's carriage.
But you'll join 'em all of course, and stand poor Mr. Lambert's friend;
I'll look in twice a day, just to see, like, how they mend.
To be sure it is a sight that might draw tears from dogs and cats;
Here's this pretty little pagoda, now has lost four of its cocked hats:
Be particular with the pagoda: and then here's this pretty bowl –
The Chinese Prince is making love to nothing because of this hole;
And here's another Chinese man, with a face just like a doll –
Do stick his pigtail on again, and just mend his parasol.
But I needn't tell you what to do; only do it out of hand,
And charge whatever you like to charge – my Lady won't make a stand.
Well! good morning, Mr. What-d'ye-call; for it's time our gossip ended:
And you know the proverb, the less as is said, the sooner the Chiny's mended.

George Colman the Younger (1762–1836)

67

Monody on a Tea-kettle

O Muse who sangest late another's pain,
To griefs domestic turn thy coal-black steed!
With slowest steps thy funeral steed must go,
Nodding his head in all the pomp of woe:
Wide scatter round each dark and deadly weed,
And let the melancholy dirge complain,
(Whilst Bats shall shriek and Dogs shall howling run)
The tea kettle is spoilt and Coleridge is undone!

Your cheerful songs, ye unseen crickets, cease!
Let songs of grief your alter'd minds engage!
For he who sang responsive to your lay,
What time the Joyous bubbles 'gan to play,
The *sooty swain* has felt the fire's fierce rage; –
Yes, he is gone, and all my woes increase;
I heard the water issuing from the wound –
No more the Tea shall pour its fragrant steams around!

O Goddess best belov'd: Delightful Tea!
With thee compar'd what yields the madd'ning Vine?
Sweet power! who know'st to spread the calm delight,
And the pure joy prolong to midmost night!
Ah! must I all thy varied sweets resign?
Enfolded close in grief thy form I see;
No more wilt thou extend thy willing arms,
Receive the *fervent Joys*, and yield him all thy charms!

How sink the mighty low by Fate opprest! –
Perhaps, O Kettle! thou by scornful toe
Rude urg'd t'ignoble place with plaintive din,
May'st rust obscure midst heaps of vulgar tin; –
As if no joy had ever seiz'd my breast
When from thy spout the streams did arching fly, –
As if, infus'd, thou ne'er hadst known t'inspire
All the warm raptures of poetic fire!

But hark! or do I fancy the glad voice –
'What tho' the swain did wondrous charms disclose –
(Not such did Memnon's sister sable drest)
Take these bright arms with royal face imprest,
A better Kettle shall thy soul rejoice,
And with Oblivion's wings o'erspread thy woes!'
Thus Fairy Hope can soothe distress and toil;
On empty Trivets she bids fancied Kettles boil!

Samuel Taylor Coleridge (1772–1834)
(First published 1834)

68

Inscription for a Coffee Pot (1830)

A golden medal was voted to me
By a certain Royal Society:
'Twas not a thing at which to scoff,
For fifty guineas was the cost thereof:
On one side a head of the king you might see,
And on the other was Mercury!
But I was scant of worldly riches,
And moreover the Mercury had no breeches;
So, thinking of honour and utility too,
And having modesty also in view,
I sold this medal (why should I not?)
And with the money for it I got
I purchased this silver coffee-pot:
Which I trust my son will preserve with care,
To be handed down from heir to heir.
These verses are engraven here,
That the truth of the matter may appear,
And I hope the society will be so wise,
As in future to dress their Mercuries!

Robert Southey (1774–1843)

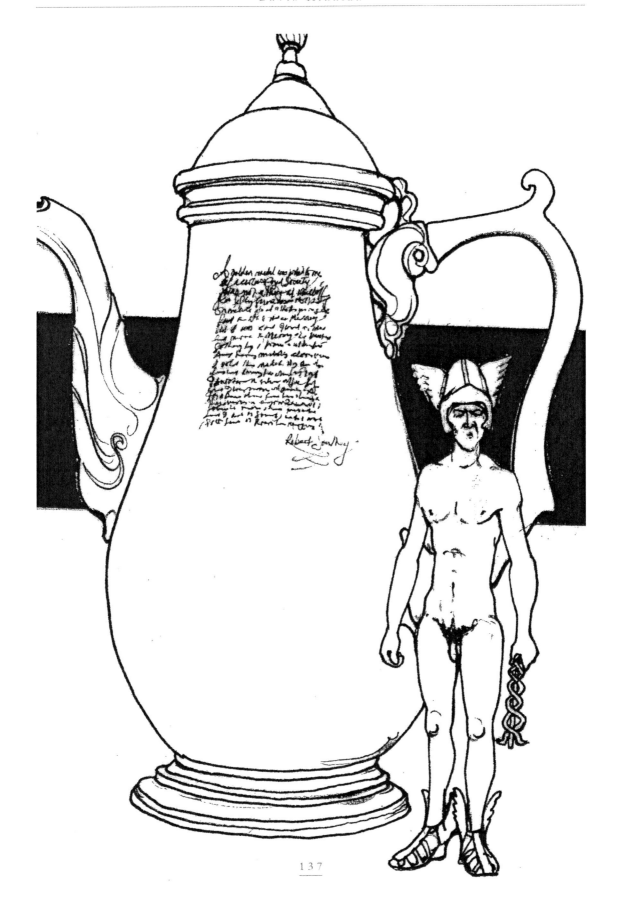

69

Letter to Maria Gisborne

And in this bowl of quicksilver – for I
Yield to the impulse of an infancy
Outlasting manhood – I have made to float
A rude idealism of a paper boat: –
A hollow screw with cogs – Henry will know
The thing I mean and laugh at me, – if so
He fears not I should do more mischief. – Next
Lie bills and calculations much perplexed,
With steam-boats, frigates, and machinery quaint
Traced over them in blue and yellow paint.
Then comes a range of mathematical
Instruments, for plans nautical and statical;
A heap of rosin, a queer broken glass
With ink in it; – a china cup that was
What it will never be again, I think, –
A thing from which sweet lips were wont to drink
The liquor doctors rail at – and which I
Will quaff in spite of them – and when we die
We'll toss up who died first of drinking tea,
And cry out, – 'Heads or tails?' where'er we be.
Near that a dusty paint-box, some odd hooks,
A half-burnt match, an ivory block, three books,
Where conic sections, spherics, logarithms,
To great Laplace, from Saunderson and Sims,
Lie heaped in their harmonious disarray
Of figures, – disentangle them who may.
Baron de Tott's Memoirs beside them lie,
And some odd volumes of old chemistry.
Near those a most inexplicable thing,
With lead in the middle – I'm conjecturing
How to made Henry understand; but no –
I'll leave, as Spenser says, with many mo,
This secret in the pregnant womb of time,
Too vast a matter for so weak a rhyme.

Percy Bysshe Shelley (1792–1822)

70

On the Bust of Helen
By Canova (1816)

In this beloved marble view,
Above the works and thought of man,
What nature *could* but *would not*, do,
And beauty and Canova *can*!
Beyond imagination's power,
Beyond the Bard's defeated art,
With immortality her dower,
Behold the *Helen* of *the heart*!

George Gordon, Lord Byron (1788–1824)

Byron wrote: 'The Helen of Canova (a bust which is in the house of Madame the Countess d'Albrizzi) is, without exception, to my mind, the most perfectly beautiful of human conceptions, and far beyond my ideas of human execution.'

71

Song of the Goblet

I have kept my place at the rich man's board
For many a waning night;
Where streams of dazzling splendour poured
Their galaxy of light:
No wilder revelry has rung
Than where my home has been;
All that the bard of Teos sung,
Has the golden Goblet seen:
And what I could tell, full many might deem
A fable of fancy, or tale of a dream.

I have beheld a courteous band
Sit round in bright array;
Their voices firm, their words all bland,
And brows like a cloudless day:
But soon the guests were led by the host
To dash out Reason's lamp;
And then GOD's noble image had lost
The fineness of its stamp:
And their sober cheeks have blushed to hear
What they told o'er me without shame or fear.

Their loud and tuneless laugh would tell
Of a hot and reeling brain;
Their right arms trembled, and red wine fell
Like blood on a battle-plain.
The youth would play the chattering ape,
And the gray-haired one would let
The foul and sickening jest escape
Till I've loathed the lips I've met;
And the swine in the dust, or the wolf on its prey,
Gave less of sheer disgust than they.

The drunkard has filled me again and again
'Mid the roar of a frantic din;
Till the starting eyeballs told his brain
Was an Etna pile within.
Oh! sad is the work that I have done
In the hands of the sot and fool;
Cursèd and dark is the fame I have won,
As Death's most powerful tool:
And I own that those who greet my rim
Too oft, will find their bane of the brim.

But all the golden Goblet has wrought
Is not the evil kind;
I have helped the creature of mighty thought,
And quickened the Godlike mind.
As gems of first water may lie in the shade,
And no lustre be known to live;
Till the kiss of the noontide beam has betrayed
What a glorious sheen they can give:
So, the breast may hold fire that none can see,
Till it meet the sun-ray shed by me.

I have burst the spirit's moody trance,
And woke it to mirth and wit;
Till the soul would dance in every glance
Of eyes that were rapture-lit.
I have heard the bosom all warm and rife
With friendship, offer up
Its faith in heaven, its hope on earth,
With the name it breathed in the cup!
And I was proud to seal the bond
Of the truly great and the firmly fond.

I have served to raise the shivering form
That sunk in the driving gale;
I have fanned the flame that famine and storm
Had done their worst to pale.
The stagnant vein has been curdled and cold
As the marble's icy streak;
But I have come, and the tide hath rolled
Right on to the heart and cheek;
And bursting words from a grateful breast
Have told the golden Goblet was blest.

Oh! Heaven forbid that bar or ban
Should be thrown on the draught I bear.
But woeful it is that senseless man
Will brand me with sin and despair.
Use me wisely, and I will lend
A joy ye may cherish and praise;
But love me too well, and my potion shall send
A burning blight on your days.
This is the strain I sing as ye fill –
"Beware! the Goblet can cheer or kill."

Eliza Cook (1818–89)

72

On a Nankin Plate

'Ah no, but it might have been!
Was there ever so dismal a fate?' –
Quoth the little blue mandarin.

'Such a maid was never seen!
She passed, tho' I cried to her "Wait," –
Ah me, but it might have been.

'I cried "O my Flower, my Queen,
Be mine!" 'Twas precipitate,' –
Quoth the little blue mandarin, –

'But then ... she was just sixteen, –
Long-eyed, as a lily straight, –
Ah me, but it might have been!

'As it was, from her palankeen,
She laughed – "You're a week too late!"
(Quoth the little blue mandarin.)

'That is why, in a mist of spleen,
I mourn on this Nankin Plate.
Ah me, but it might have been!'
Quoth the little blue mandarin.

Austin Dobson (1840–1921)

73

Lines Inscribed Upon a Cup Formed from a Skull (1808)

Start not – nor deem my spirit fled:
In me behold the only skull,
From which, unlike a living head,
Whatever flows is never dull.

I lived, I loved, I quaff'd , like thee;
I died: let earth my bones resign:
Fill up – thou canst not injure me;
The worm hath fouler lips than thine.

Better to hold the sparkling grape,
Than nurse the earth-worm's slimy brood;
And circle in the goblet's shape
The drink of gods, than reptiles' food.

Where once my wit, perchance, hath shone,
In aid of others' let me shine;
And when, alas! our brains are gone,
What nobler substitute than wine?

Quaff while thou canst: another race,
When thou and thine like me are sped,
May rescue thee from earth's embrace,
And rhyme and revel with the dead.

Why not? since through life's little day
Our heads such sad effects produce;
Redeem'd from worms and wasting clay,
This chance is theirs, to be of use.

George Gordon, Lord Byron (1788–1824)

74

On Seeing the Elgin Marbles
for the First Time

My spirit is too weak; mortality
Weighs heavily on me like unwilling sleep,
And each imagined pinnacle and steep
Of godlike hardship tells me I must die
Like a sick eagle looking at the sky.
Yet 'tis a gentle luxury to weep,
That I have not the cloudy winds to keep
Fresh for the opening of the morning's eye.
Such dim-conceivèd glories of the brain
Bring round the heart and indescribable feud;
So do these wonders a most dizzy pain,
What mingles Grecian grandeur with the rude
Wasting of old Time – with a billowy main
A sun, a shadow of a magnitude.

John Keats (1795–1821)

75

An Irish Folksong

My Aunt she died a month ago
She left me all her riches,
A feather bed, a wooden leg,
A pair of calico breeches.

A coffee pot without a spout,
A mug without a handle
A baccy box without a lid
And half a farthing candle.

Anon.

76

Nick-nackets

(from 'Captain Grose's Pereginations – through the Highlands')

He had a rowth o' auld nick-nackets,
Rusty airn cups and jinglin'-jackets
Would hold the Loudons three in tackets
A towmond gude;
And parritch-pots and auld saut-buckets,
Afore the flude.

Robert Burns (1759–1796)

77

A Squib on Sir William Hamilton

The world, reports (I hope untrue)
That half Sir William's mugs and gods are new;
Himself the baker of th'Etrurian ware
That made our British antiquarians stare.

'PETER PINDAR' (John Walcot 1773–1819)

Sir William Hamilton, the husband of Nelson's Emma, was British Plenipotentiary at the Court of Naples. He was one of the first Englishmen to appreciate and collect Greek vases, and the printed catalogues of his collections (1766 and 1767, 1791 and 1795) influenced Wedgwood – whose factory in Staffordshire was called Etruria – and the styles of Flaxman and Fuseli.

78

Roman Antiquities Discovered at Bishopstone, Herefordshire published 1835

While poring Antiquarians search the ground
Upturned with curious pains, the Bard, a Seer,
Takes fire:– The men that have been reappear;
Romans for travel girt, for business gowned;
And some recline on couches, myrtle-crowned,
In festal glee: why not? For fresh and clear,
As if its hues were of the passing year,
Dawns this time-buried pavement. From that mound
Hoards may come forth of Trajans, Maximins,
Shrunk into coins with all their warlike toil;
Or a fierce impress issues with its foil
Of tenderness – the Wolf, whose suckling Twins
The unlettered ploughboy pities when he wins
The casual treasure from the furrowed soil.

William Wordsworth (1770–1850)

79

On a Painting by Julius Olsson R.A.

Over what bridge-fours has that luscious sea
Shone sparkling from its frame of bronzèd gold
Since waves of foaming opalescence roll'd
One warm spring morning, back in twenty-three,
All through the day, from breakfast-time till tea,
When Julius Olsson, feeling rather cold,
Packed up his easel and, contented, stroll'd
Back to St. Ives, its fisher-folk and quay.

Over what bridge-parties, cloche-hat, low waist,
Has looked that seascape, once so highly-prized,
From Lenygon-green walls, until, despised –
'It isn't art. It's only just a knack' –
It fell from grace. Now, in a change of taste,
See Julius Olsson slowly strolling back.

John Betjeman (1906–84)

80

The Poet's Furniture

This wheel-footed, studying chair,
Contriv'd both for toil and repose,
Wide-elbow'd, and wadded with hair,
In which I both scribble and dose,
Bright-studded to dazzle the eyes,
And rival in lustre of that
In which, or astronomy lies,
Fair Cassiopeia sat:

These carpets, so soft to the foot,
Caledonia's traffic and pride!
Oh spare them, ye knight of the boot,
Escap'd from a cross-country ride!
This table and mirror within,
Secure from collision and dust,
At which I oft shave cheek and chin,
And periwig nicely adjust:

This moveable structure of shelves,
For its beauty admired and its use,
And charged with octavos and twelves,
The gayest I had to produce;
Where, flaming in scarlet and gold,
My poems enchanted I view,
And hope, in due time, to behold
My Iliad and Odyssey too:

This china, that decks the alcove,
Which people here all call a buffet,
But what the gods call it above,
Has ne'er been revealed to us yet:
These curtains, that keep the room warm
Or cool as the season demands,
Those stoves that for pattern and form,
Seem the labour of Mulciber's hands.

William Cowper (1731–1800)

81

The Metamorphosis, or Toby reduc'd.

Dear Tome, this brown Jug that now foams with mild Ale,
(In which I will drink to sweet Nan of the Vale),
Was once Toby Fillpot, a thirsty old Soul
As e'er drank a Bottle or fathom'd a Bowl.
In boozing about 'twas his praise to excell,
And among Jolly Topers he bore off the Bell.

It chanc'd as in Dog-days he sat at his ease,
In his Flow'r-woven Arbour as gay as you please,
With a Friend and a Pipe, puffing Sorrow away
And with honest old Stingo was soaking his Clay,
His breath Doors of Life on a sudden were shut
And he died full as big as a Dorchester Butt.

His Body, when long in the Ground it had lain
And time into Clay had resolv'd it again
A Potter found out in its Covert so snug
And with part of fat Toby he form'd this brown Jug
Now sacred to Friendship and Mirth and mild Ale.
So here's to my lovely sweet Nan of the Vale.

Francis Fawkes (1720–77)

It is now generally believed that the name of the Toby jug derives from this poem, which was first printed in 1761 in Fawkes's volume of *Original Poems and Translations*. The poem became popular through its reprinting beneath an engraving, published by Carrington Bowles after a design by Robert Dighton, which showed a jovial toper with bulging paunch, foaming tankard and church-warden pipe. At Covent Garden, in 1783, the poem was introduced by John O'Keefe into his comic opera The *Poor Soldier*. It was subsequently sung with success by John Johnstone and Charles Incledon and was even quoted by Canning in the House of Commons during a debate on Catholic Emancipation. (See John Hadfield, 'The Surprising History of The Fillpot Family', *The Saturday Book*, IX 1949, p. 147.)

82

A Case of Cameos

AGATE
(The Power of Love)
First, in an Agate-stone, a Centaur strong,
With square man-breasts and hide of dapple dun,
His brown arms bound behind him with a thong,
On strained croup strove to free himself from one, –
A bolder rider than Bellerophon.
For, on his back, by some strange power of art,
There sat a laughing Boy with bow and dart,
Who drave him where he would, and driving him,
With that barbed toy would make him rear and start.
To this was writ 'World-victor' on the rim.

CHALCEDONY
(The Thefts of Mercury)
The next in legend bade 'Beware of show!'
'Twas graven thus on pale Chalcedony.
Here great Apollo, with unbended bow,
His quiver hard by on a laurel tree,
For some new theft was rating Mercury.
Who stood with downcast eyes, and feigned distress,
As daring not, for utter guiltiness,
To meet that angry voice and aspect joined.
His very heel-wings drooped; but yet, not less,
His backward hand the Sun-God's shafts purloined.

SARDONYX
(The Song of Orpheus)
Then, on a Sardonyx, the man of Thrace,
The voice supreme that through Hell's portals stole,
With carved white lyre and glorious song-lit face,
(Too soon, alas! on Hebrus' wave to roll!)
Played to the beasts, from a great elm-tree bole.
And lo! with half-shut eyes the leopard spread
His lissome length; and deer with gentle tread
Came through the trees; and, from a nearer spring,
The prick-eared rabbit paused; while overhead
The stock-dove drifted downward, fluttering.

AMETHYST
(The Crowning of Silenus)
Next came an Amethyst – the grape in hue.
On a mock throne, by fresh excess disgraced,
With heavy head, and thyrsus held askew,
The Youths, in scorn, had dull Silenus placed,
And o'er him 'King of Topers' they had traced.
Yet but a King of Sleep he seemed at best,
With wine-bag cheeks that bulged upon his breast,
And vat-like paunch distent from his carouse.
Meanwhile, his ass, by no respect represt,
Munched at the wreath upon her Master's brows.

BERYL
(The Sirens)
Lastly, with 'Pleasure' was a Beryl graven,
Clear-hued, divine. Thereon the Sirens sung.
What time, beneath, by rough rock-bases caven,
And jaw-like rifts where many a green bone clung
The strong flood-tide, in-rushing, coiled and swung.
Then, – in the offing, – on the lift of the sea,
A tall ship drawing shoreward – helplessly.
For, from the prow, e'en now the rowers leap
Headlong, nor seek from that sweet fate to flee ...
Ah me, those Women-witches of the Deep!

Austin Dobson (1840–1921)

83

Ode on the Death of a Favourite Cat Drowned in a Tub of Gold Fishes

Twas on this lofty vase's side,
Where China's gayest art had dyed
The azure flowers, that blow;
Demurest of the tabby kind,
The pensive Selima, reclined,
Gazed on the lake below.

Her conscious tail her joy declared;
The fair round face, the snowy beard,
The velvet of her paws,
Her coat that with the tortoise vies,
Her ears of jet, and emerald eyes,
She saw; and purr'd applause.

Still had she gazed; but 'midst the tide
Two angel forms were seen to glide,
The Genii of the stream:
Their scaly armour's Tyrian hue
Through richest purple to the view
Betray'd a golden gleam.

The hapless nymph with wonder saw:
A whisker first and then a claw,
With many an ardent wish,
She stretch'd, in vain, to reach the prize
What female heart can gold despise?
What Cat's averse to fish?

Presumptuous maid! with looks intent
Again she stretch'd, again she bent,
Nor knew the gulf between.
(Malignant Fate sat by, and smiled)
The slipp'ry verge her feet beguiled,
She tumbled headlong in.

Eight times emerging from the flood
She mew'd to ev'ry wat'ry God,
Some speedy aid to send.
No Dolphin came, no Nereid stirr'd:
Nor cruel Tom, nor Susan heard.
A fav'rite has no friend!

From hence, ye beauties, undeceived,
Know, one false step is ne'er retrieved,
And be with caution bold.
Not all that tempts your wand'ring eyes
And heedless hearts is lawful prize,
Nor all, that glisters, gold.

Thomas Gray (1716–71)

The cat belonged to Horace Walpole; and the china vase was one of the most prized pieces in his collection. It is described in the 1784 catalogue of Strawberry Hill as '*The celebrated large blue and white* ORIENTAL CHINA CISTERN, on Gothic carved pedestal, *in which* HORACE WALPOLE's cat *was drowned*, this gave occasion to Mr. Gray, the poet, to write his beautiful Ode, beginning thus:

"'Twas on this lofty vase's side ... & etc.'"

Walpole had a special label printed with Gray's poem at the Strawberry Hill Press. At the 1842 sale the cistern was bought by the Earl of Derby for £42, and it is still at Knowsley, in spite of the suggestion by Mr. Edmund Blunden, in a letter to the Editor of the *Times Literary Supplement*, that 'cat-lovers everywhere are no doubt waiting to trace and in contemporary fashion to annihilate this relic of medieval barbarism, and no doubt Chinese torture!'

84

On a Fan that Belonged to the Marquise de Pompadour

Chicken-skin, delicate, white,
Painted, by Carlo Vanloo,
Loves in a riot of light,
Roses and vaporous blue;
Hark to the dainty *frou-frou*!
Picture above, if you can,
Eyes that could melt as the dew, –
This was the Pompadour's fan!

See how they rise at the sight.
Thronging the *Oeil de Boeuf* through,
Courtiers as butterflies bright,
Beauties that Fragonard drew,
Talon-rouge, falbala, queue,
Cardinal, Duke, – to a man,
Eager to sigh or to sue, –
This was the Pompadour's fan!

Ah, but things more than polite
Hung on this toy, *voyez-vous*!
Matters of state and of might,
Things that great ministers do;
Things that, maybe, overthrew
Those in whose brains they began;
Here was the sign and the cue, –
This was the Pompadour's fan!

ENVOY
Where are the secrets it knew?
Weavings of plot and of plan?
– But where is the Pompadour, too?
This was the Pompadour's *fan*!

Austin Dobson (1840–1921)

85

Isabella; or, The Morning (1740)

To please the noble dame, the courtly 'squire
Produced a *tea pot*, made in Staffordshire:
With eager eyes the longing Duchess stood,
and o'er and o'er the shining bauble view'd:
Such were the joys touched young Atrides' breast,
Such all the Grecian host at once exprest,
When from beneath his robe, to all their view,
Laertes' son the fam'd Palladium drew.
So Venus look'd, and with such longing eyes,
When Paris first produc'd the golden prize.
'Such work as this,' she cries, 'can England do?
It equals Dresden, and outdoes St. Cloud:
All modern China now shall hide its head,
And e'en Chantilly must give o'er the trade:
For lace let Flanders bear away the bell
In finest linen let the Dutch excel;
For prettiest stuffs let Ireland first be nam'd,
And for best-fancy'd silks let France be fam'd;
Do thou, thrice-happy England! still prepare
This clay, and build the same on Earthenware.'
More she'd have said, but that again she heard
The knocker – and the General appear'd....

'Your servant, Sir – but see what I have got!
Isn't it a prodigious charming *pot*?
And a'n't you vastly glad we make them here?
For Dicky got it out of Staffordshire.
See how the charming vine twines all about!
Lord! what a handle! Jesus! what a spout!
And that old Pagog, and that charming child!
If Lady Townshend saw them, she'd be wild!'

To this the Gen'ral: 'Madam, who would not?
Lord! where could Mr. Bateman find this *pot*?
Dear Dicky, cou'dn't you get one for me?
I want some useful china mightily;
Two jars, two beakers, and a *pot-pourri*.'

Sir Charles Hanbury-Williams (1708-59)

The main character of this piece is Isabella, Duchess of Manchester (1692–1786). The 'courtly squire' is Richard Bateman (brother of Viscount Bateman), whose collection was sold by Christie's in May 1774. The Lady Townshend mentioned is Audrey Harrison, only daughter of Edward Harrison of Balls, Hertfordshire; she was wife of Charles, third Viscount Townshend, and mother of George, first Marquis of Townshend, and of Charles Townshend. The General was General Churchill, son of a brother of the great Duke of Marlborough.

86

Prologue (to Taste; A Comedy of Two Acts by Samuel Foote, 1753)

Written by MR. GARRICK and spoken by him in the Character of an Auctioneer.

Before this Court I PETER PUFF appear,
A Briton born, and bred an Auctioneer;
Who for myself, and eke a hundred others,
My useful, honest, learned, brawling Brothers,
With much Humility and Fear implore ye,
To lay our present, desp'rate Case before ye.
'Tis said this Night a certain Wag intends
To laugh at us, our Calling, and our Friends:
If Lords and Ladies, and such dainty Folks,
Are cur'd of Auction-hunting by his Jokes;
Should this odd Doctrine spread throughout the Land
Before you buy, be sure to understand,
Oh! think on us what various Ills will flow,
When great Ones only purchase – what they know.
Why laugh at TASTE? It is a harmless Fashion,
And quite subdues each detrimental Passion;
The Fair ones' Hearts will ne'er incline to Man,
While thus they rage for – China and Japan.
The Virtuoso too, and Connoisseur,
As ever decent, delicate and pure;
The smallest Hair their looser Thoughts might hold,
Just warm when Single, and when Married cold:
Their Blood at Sight of Beauty gently flows;
Their Venus must be old, and want a Nose!
No am'rous Passion with deep Knowledge thrives;
'Tis the Complaint indeed of all our Wives!
'Tis said Virtu to such a Heighth is grown,
All Artists are encourag'd – but our own.
Be not deceiv'd, I here declare on Oath,
I never yet sold Goods of foreign Growth:
Ne'er sent Commissions out to Greece or Rome;
My best Antiques are made at Home.
I've Romans, Greeks, Italians near at hand,
True Britons all – and living in the Strand.

I ne'er for Trinkets rack my Pericranium,
They furnish out my Room from Herculaneum.
But hush –

Should it be known that English are employ'd,
Our Manufacture is at once destroy'd;
No matter what our Countrymen deserve,
They'll thrive as Antients, but as Moderns starve –
If we should fall – to you it will be owing;
Farewell to Arts – they're going, going, going;
The fatal Hammer's in your Hand, oh Town!
Then set Us up – and knock the POET down.

David Garrick (1717–79)

87

The Fan

I singe that graceful toy, whose waving play
With gentle gales relieves the sultry day.
Not the wide fan by Persian dames display'd,
Which o'er their beauty casts a grateful shade;
Not that long known in China's artful land,
Which while it cools the face, fatigues the hand:
Nor shall the muse in Asian climates rove,
To seek in Indostan some spicy grove,
Where stretch'd at ease the panting lady lies,
To shun the fervour of meridian skies,
While sweating slaves catch ev'ry breeze of air,
And with wide-spreading fans refresh the fair;
No busy gnats her pleasing dreams molest,
Inflame her cheek, or ravage o'er her breast,
But artificial zephyrs round her fly,
And mitigate the fever of the sky...

A different toil another forge employs:
Here the loud hammer fashions female toys,
Hence in the fair with ornaments supplied,
Hence sprung the glitt'ring implements of pride;
Each trinket that adorns the modern dame,
First to those little artists owed its frame.
Here an unfinish'd di'mond crosslet lay
To which soft lovers adoration pay;
There was the polish'd crystal bottle seen,
That with quick scents revives the modish spleen:
Here the yet rude unjointed snuff-box lies,
Which serves the rallied fop for smart replies;
There piles of paper rose in gilded reams,
The future records of the lover's flames;
Here clouded canes midst heaps of toys are found,
And inlaid tweezer-cases strow the ground.
There stands the Toilette, nursery of charms,
Completely furnish'd with bright beauty's arms:
The patch, the powder-box, pulville, perfumes,
Pins, paints, a flatt'ring glass, and black-lead combs...

Industrious Loves, your present toils forbear,
A more important task demands your care:
Long has the scheme employ'd my thoughtful mind,
By judgment ripen'd, and by time refined.
That glorious bird have ye not often seen
Who draws the car of the celestial Queen?
Have ye not oft survey'd his varying dyes,
His tail all gilded o'er with Argus' eyes?
Have ye not seen him in the sunny day
Unfurl his plumes, and all his pride display,
Then suddenly contract his dazzling train,
And with long-trailing feathers sweep the plain?
Learn from this hint, let this instruct your art:
Thin taper sticks must form one centre part;
Let these into the quandrant's form divide,
The spreading ribs with snowy paper hide;
Here shall the pencil bid its colours flow,
And make a minature creation grow.
Let the machine in equal foldings close,
And now its plaited surface wide dispose.
So shall the fair her idle hand employ,
And grace each motion with the restless toy,
With various play bid grateful Zephyrs rise,
While love in ev'ry grateful Zephyr flies.

John Gay (1685–1732)

88

On Dan Jackson's Picture Cut in Paper

To fair Lady *Betty*[9] *Dan*[10] sat for his Picture,
And defy'd her to draw him so oft as he piqu'd her.
He knew she'd no Pencil or Colouring by her,
And therefore he thought he might safely defy her.
Come sit, says my Lady, then whips up her Scissar
And cuts out his Coxcomb in Silk in a trice, Sir.
Dan sat with Attention, and saw with Surprize
How she lengthen'd his Chin, how she hollow'd his Eyes,
But flatter'd himself with a secret Conceit,
That his thin leathern Jaws all her Art would defeat.
Lady *Betty* observ'd it, then pulls out a Pin,
And varies the Grain of the Stuff to his Grin;
And to make roasted Silk to resemble his raw-bone,
She rais'd up a Thread to the jett of his Jaw-bone,
Till at length, in exactest Proportion he rose,
From the Crown of his Head to the Arch of his Nose,
And if Lady *Betty* had drawn him with Wig and all,
'Tis certain the Copy had out-done the Original,
Well, that's but my Outside, says Dan with a Vapour;
Say you so? says my Lady; I've lin'd it with Paper,

Jonathan Swift (1667–1745)

[9] *Lady Betty.* The wife of George Rochfort.
[10] The Rev. Daniel Jackson was a cousin of Robert and John Grattan, with whom Swift was in the habit of exchanging verses, Jackson's large nose was a constant subject of jest in the circle of Swift's friends and is mentioned in several verse trifles.

89

The Tea-pot or the Lady's Transformation

Soft *Venus*, Love's too anxious Queen
In fit of Vapours or of Spleen,
Because, perhaps, a fav'rite God
Fail'd to return her *smile* or *nod*,
Or that Her Mars of late grown cold,
Behav'd less kindly than of old,
With inward sullen discontent,
To *Juno* utter'd this Complaint.
'There lives a Nymph below the Skies,
'That Carries *Witchcraft* in her Eyes,
'No fond Addresses will she take
'From lovers of a *Mortal* make:
'But turns her haughty looks above
'Perhaps to *Mars*, perhaps to *Jove*:
'Disdaining Men she seems to mark
'None less than in Ætherial Spark,
'And oft' you know we've born Disgrace,
'Despised for those of *Human Race*,
'If more such Nymphs get leave to reign,
'Our Empire we shall ne'er maintain,
'But Goddesses resign their Birth,
'To the bright *Morts* who ply on Earth.'

So *Venus* spoke with Envy fir'd –
The other Jealousie inspir'd,
And red with Rage, and big with Hate,
She thus pronounc'd the Virgin's fate,
'She whose aspiring thoughts can rise
'To Tempt a Rival in the Skies,
'Who thus with Stubborn Pride neglects,
Th'Addresses of the kindred *Sex*,
Into a Tea-pot's Figure thrown
'Shall still attend and serve her own.'

When now her doom was fix'd, the Maid
Before a Glass her Form survey'd
Her eyes that o'er her Beauties range
Too soon perceive the fatal Change:
She sees, she feels the dire Decay;
Grows cold and stiffens into Clay;
Extinguish'd lye the vital Fires,
And every crimson Blush retires.
The well turn'd Waste in Canvas bound,
Shrunk to a little hollow round:

The Iv'ry Arm that in her side
By chance she plac'd with comely Pride,
By Fate was in that Posture held
And in a Handle's form congeal'd —
Amaz'd with Horror and Surprise
She lifts to Heaven her Wat'ry Eyes;
Unpitying Heaven – and Oh! She cry'd —
Her Mouth grew circular and wide
Her lips, that once outvied the Rose,
Turn pale and in a Cover Close.

Her Tongue, which last in Health remain'd,
And last its Suppleness retain'd,
With usual Pliance nimbly skips
To feel the Change between her Lips,
But losing there all Power to move,
Appears a little knob above,
Which Helps as formerly to hide,
Seldom to hide th'interior Side.

But what was chang'd into the Spout,
The curious Muse resolves with Doubt.
Uncertain whether 'twere the Nose,
Because from thence a Liquid flows,
Or Eyes because they oft' reveal'd
What hidden things the Lips conceal'd —
Howe'er it was, by *Juno's* hands,
The Nymph a finish'd Teapot stands.

Now from the High Caelestial Plain
The goddesses Cofederate lean,
And with Malitious Triumph they
Their Monument of Wrath Survey:
Upon a stricter View they find
Some Parts remain unchang'd behind,
And with those Relicts of their Rage,
They furnish out an Equipage —
Part of the Scull, well temper'd Clay,
Fell off and in a Slop-Dish lay:
Her polish'd Forehead being thought
Good Metal, into Spoons was wrought.
Holes in the Heart where Secrets lay,
Became Receptacles for Tea,
The Tea as Secrets did of old
Drops out again before 'tis cold.
Her lungs another Form receive
And in respiring Bellows heave;
The Bellows still delight to blow
Coals that beneath the Kettle Glow.

Ambrose Philips (c.1675–1749)

Pasted into the same British Museum book of pamphlets is another broadsheet poem, *The Metamorphose of a Certain Dublin Beau's Head Into a TEA-KETTLE*. In this case dated 1730, it is 'By a Lady', It follows very much the same lines as 'Namby Pamby' Philips's piece. Here is an extract:

His dull vivacious Head the Goddess try'd,
Found, while a Head, it must be misapply'd.
Resolv'd, to make it now her firmest Port,
Where she might harbour, and her Train resort
And now devoted to her future Rites,
The source of Verbal Wars and Female Flights,
Soon o'er his Front there spread a Brassy Hue,
Out from his Nose a hollow Pipe she drew,
His dusty Noddle-case fell round his Ears,
As Blossom's fall, when budding Fruit appears.

90

The Book-plate's Petition
by a Gentleman of the Temple

While cynic Charles still trimm'd the vane
'Twixt *Querouaille* and *Castlemaine*,
In days that shocked JOHN EVELYN,
My First Possessor fixed me in.
In days of *Dutchman* and of frost,
The narrow sea with James I cross'd,
Returning when once more began
The age of *Saturn* and of ANNE.
I am a part of all the past:
I knew the GEORGES, first and last;
I have been oft where else was none
Save the great wig of ADDISON;
And seen on shelves beneath me grope
The little eager form of POPE.
I lost the Third that owned me when
French NOAILLES fled at Dettingen;
The year JAMES WOLFE surprised Quebec
The Fourth in hunting broke his neck;
The day that WILLIAM HOGARTH dy'd
The Fifth one found me in Cheapside,
This was a *Scholar*, one of those
Whose *Greek* is sounder than their *hose*;
He lov'd old Books and nappy ale,
So liv'd at Streatham, next to THRALE.
'Twas there this stain of grease I boast
Was made by DR. JOHNSON's toast.
(He did it, as I think, for spite;
My Master call'd him Jacobite!)
And now that I so long to-day
Have rested *post discrimina*.
Safe in the brass-wir'd book-case where
I watch'd the Vicar's whit'ning hair,
Must I those travell'd bones inter
In some *Collector's* sepulchre!
Must I be torn herefrom and thrown
With *frontispiece* and *colophon*!

With vagrant E's, and I's, and O's,
The spoil of plunder'd *Folios*!
With scraps and snippets that to ME
Are naught but *kitchen company*!
Nay, rather, FRIEND, this favour grant me:
Tear me at once, *but don't transplant me.*
Cheltenham. September 31, 1792.

Austin Dobson (1840–1921)

91

The Broken Mug

Quem saepe transit, Casus aliquando invenit

This MUG which I lament in Tears
Hath serv'd me well for many Years;
That useful piece of Furniture
Is broke and batter'd past all Cure;
Nor can it e'er be Hoop'd with Tin,
As other broken MUGS have been,
Where *Ruptures* cur'd by Tinker's Truss
Are still of special Use to us.

But now alas! 'tis all in vain
To join the particle again.
What Cost wou'd I on thee bestow,
To have thee now in *Statu Quo*?
Thou MUG the Subject of my Song,
Should not lye still or empty long.
In Silver Hoops you should appear
Well Tipp'd, and frothing full of *Beer*,
Whose fragrant Bubbles gently fall,
Till by Degrees contracted small,
They on the centre form a Rose
So grateful to our Eyes and Nose,
Whose mantling Juice doth far out-shine
The sparkling of the choicest Wine.

It was a Family old MUG,
At which our Friends did often Tug:
'Twas bought when I was but a Youth,
And *Granny* says, Upon her Truth,
A finer MUG was never bought,
Altho' it cost her but a *Groat*.

I guess'd my brother Bards were dry
Then begg'd a Nimph who lives hard by,
To step to Hellicon in Haste,
And bring the MUG full of the Best.
In Haste did she Trip down the Stairs

It serv'd a double 'Prenticeship,
And never got a Crack or Slip,
Until by Chance the other Day,
To shew the Frailty of our Clay,
It got a most unlucky Fall,
Which may be Warning to us all:
For let us live to *Nestor's* Age,
We must at last go off the Stage.

'Twas made in ANNA's Glorious Reign,
And always kept both sweet and clean;
Her Health was often Drank thereout,
In *March* or in *October* STOUT...
Tho' now the *Mode*, 'tis not my Way
To entertain my Friends with TEA;
We Bards don't love our Drink too New,
Nor can we spare the Time to Brew;
We drink no Tea or Coffee here,
They're both insipid and too dear;
They never can clear up the Brain
Or put me in a merry Vein.
To some they give ill-natur'd Fits,
While base Detractors pass for Wits,
From whose vile Censures none are free
And all's Condemn'd by their Decree.

With graceful Air, but unawares
Precipitating on her Hoop
As she run downwards made her stoop.
Down fell the Nimph, the MUG and all,
The Loss was great and great the Fall.
The *Nimph* return'd with nimble Foot
But got her Finger sorely Cut;
The Tydings told with panting Breath,
How she escap'd a sudden Death.
The Scatter'd Limbs, O dire Mishap!
She brought up gather'd in her lap,
With fractures of the MUG so small,
No art could e'er Cement them all.

Thou best of MUGS for e'er adieu
Since I am doom'd to follow you:
I am but *Clay*, and so wert *Thou*:
When I go off, or *Where* or *How*,
I cannot tell, but still must strive
To keep this *Microcosm* alive:
So wet my *Clay* as it grows Dry,
Lest it should into *Atoms* fly.

Laurence Whyte, Dublin, 1742

92

A True and Faithful Inventory of the Goods Belonging to Dr. Swift, Vicar of Lara Cor; Upon Lending his House to the Bishop of Meath, until his own was Built

An Oaken, broken, Elbow-Chair;
A Cawdle-Cup, without an Ear;
A batter'd shatter'd Ash Bedstead;
A Box of Deal, without a Lid;
A Pair of Tongs, but out of Joint;
A Back-Sword Poker, without a Point;
A Pot that's crack'd a-cross, around,
With an old knotted Garter bound;
An Iron Lock, without a Key;
A Wig, with hanging, quite grown grey;
A Curtain worn to Half a Stripe;
A Pair of Bellows, without Pipe;
A Dish, which might good Meat afford Once;
An *Ovid*, and an old *Concordance*;
A Bottle Bottom, Wooden Platter,
One is for Meal, and one for Water;
There likewise is a Copper Skillet,
Which runs as fast out as you fill it;
A Candlestick, Snuff dish, and Save-all,
And thus his Household Goods you have all.
These, to your Lordship, as a Friend,
Till you have built, I freely lend:
They'll save your Lordship for a Shift;
Why not, as well as Doctor *Swift*?

Jonathan Swift (1667–1745)

93

Squib on Sir Andrew Fountaine

But Annius, crafty Seer, with ebon wand,
And well-dissembled em'rald on his hand,
False as his gems and cancer'd as his coins,
Came, cramm'd with capon, from where Pollio dines.

Alexander Pope (1688–1744)

Sir Andrew Fountaine (1676-1753) of Narford Hall, Norfolk, was an English virtuoso of the early eighteenth century. He was knighted by William III in 1699 and in 1701 accompanied Lord Macclesfield to Hanover to announce to the Elector the Act of Accession passed by the British parliament. From there he went on to Italy, buying antiques, including the maiolica which was to be the chief glory of his collection. In 1714 he made a long visit to Paris, and then again went to Italy, spending nearly three years at Rome and Florence, where he became a friend of Cosmo III, Grand Duke of Tuscany, the last of the Medici princes. He was also a great friend of Dean Swift: the Narford Library formerly contained a number of Swift's letters and of his drawings for *The Tale of a Tub*, sent to Narford for Sir Andrew's approval, but never returned. Sir Andrew made jaunts to china shops with Swift in 1710, a time when the Dean had a mild fancy for china-collecting. In 1718 he sold his collection of medals to the Earl of Pembroke to pay for an enlargement of Narford.

In 1727 he succeeded Sir Isaac Newton as Warden of the Mint. He died at Narford in 1753. He had no children, and at his death his title and collections devolved on a relative of his wife. The collections were mainly dispersed at Christie's in 1884.

94

Victorian Guitar

For David Hammond

I expected the lettering to carry
The date of the gift, a kind of christening:
This is more like the plate on a coffin.

Louisa Catherine Smith could not be light.
Far more than a maiden name
Was cancelled by him on the first night.

I believe he cannot have known your touch
Like this instrument – for clearly
John Charles did not hold with fingering –

Which is obviously a lady's:
The sound-box trim as a girl in stays,
The neck right for the smallest span.

Did you even keep track of it as a wife?
Do you know the man who has it now
Is giving it the time of its life?

Seamus Heaney (1939–2013)

Inscribed 'Belonged to Louisa Catherine Coe before her marriage to John Charles Smith, March 1852'.

95

Second-hand Bookstalls

Volumes on shelter'd stalls expanded lie,
And various sciences lure the learned eye;
The bending shelves, with pond'rous scholiasts groan,
And deep divines to modern shops unknown:
Here, like the bee, that on industrious wing
Collects the various odours of the spring,
Walkers, at leisure, learning's flowers may spoil,
Nor watch the wasting of the midnight oil,
May morals snatch from Plutarch's tatter'd page,
A mildew'd Bacon, or Stagira's sage.
Here saunt'ring 'prentices o'er Otway weep,
O'er Congreve smile or over D** sleep;
Pleased semptstresses the Lock's famed Rape unfold,
And Squirts read Garth, 'till apozens grow cold.

O Lintot, let my labours obvious lie,
Ranged on thy stall, for ev'ry curious eye;
So shall the poor these precepts gratis know,
And to my verse their future safeties owe.

John Gay (1685–1732)

96

Melting the Earl's Plate

Here's the gold cup all bossy with satyrs and saints,
And my race-bowl (now, women, no whining and plaints!)
From the paltriest spoon to the costliest thing,
We'll melt it all down for the use of the king.

Here's the chalice stamped over with sigil and cross, –
Some day we'll make up to the chapel the loss.
Now bring me my father's great emerald ring,
For I'll melt down the gold for the good of the king.

And bring me the casket my mother has got,
And the jewels that fall to my Barbara's lot;
Then dry up your eyes and do nothing but sing,
For we're helping to coin the gold for the king.

This dross we'll transmute into weapons of steel,
Tempered blades for the hand, sharpest spurs for the heel;
And when Charles, with a shout, into London we bring,
We'll be glad to remember this deed for the king.

Bring the hawk's silver bells, and the nursery spoon,
The crucible's ready – we're nothing too soon;
For I hear the horse neigh that shall carry the thing
That'll bring up a smile in the eyes of the king.

There go my old spurs, and the old silver jug, –
'Twas just for a moment a pang and a tug;
But now I am ready to dance and to sing,
To think I've thrown gold in the chest of my king.

The earrings lose shape, and the coronet too,
I feel my eyes dim with a sort of a dew.
Hurrah for the posset dish! – Everything
Shall run into bars for the use of the king.

That spoon is a sword, and this thimble a pike;
It's but a week's garret in London belike –
Then a dash at Whitehall, and the city shall ring
With the shouts of the multitude bringing the king.

George W. Thornbury (1828–76)

97

To a Missal of the Thirteenth Century

Missal of the Gothic age,
Missal with the blazoned page,
Whence, O Missal, hither come,
From what dim scriptorium?

Whose the name that wrought thee thus,
Ambrose or Theophilus,
Bending, through the waning light,
O'er thy vellum, scraped and white;

Weaving 'twixt thy rubric lines
Sprays and leaves and quaint designs;
Setting round thy border scrolled
Buds of purple and of gold?

Ah! – a wondering brotherhood,
Doubtless, by that artist stood,
Raising o'er his careful ways
Little choruses of praise;

Glad when his deft hand would paint
Strife of Sathanas and Saint,
Or in secret coign entwist
Jest of cloister humorist.

Well the worker earned his wage,
Bending o'er the blazoned page!
Tired the hand and tired the wit
Ere the final *Explicit*!

Not as ours the books of old –
Things that steam can stamp and fold,
Not as ours the books of yore –
Rows of type, and nothing more.

Then a book was still a Book,
Where a wistful man might look,
Finding something through the whole,
Beating, – like a human soul.

In that growth of day by day,
When to labour was to pray,
Surely something vital passed
To the patient page at last;

Something that one still perceives
Vaguely present in the leaves;
Something from the worker lent;
Something mute – but eloquent!

Austin Dobson (1840–1921)

98

The Sofa

I sing the Sofa, I who lately sang
Truth, Hope, and Charity, and touched with awe
The Solemn chords, and with a trembling hand,
Excap'd with pain from that adventurous flight,
Now seek repose upon an humbler theme;
The theme though humble, yet august and proud
Th'occasion O for the Fair commands the song.
Time was, when cloathing sumptuous or for use,
Save their own painted skins, our sires had none.
As yet black breeches were not; sattin smooth,
Or velvet soft, or plush with shaggy pile:
The hardy chief upon the rugged rock
Wash'd by the sea, or on the grav'ly bank
Thrown up by wintry torrents roaring loud,
Fearless of wrong, repos'd his weary strength.
Those barb'rous ages past, succeeded next
The birth-day of invention, weak at first,
Dull in design, and clumsy to perform.
Joint-stools were then created; on three legs
Upborne they stood. Three legs upholding firm
A massy slab, in fashion square or round.
On such a stool immortal Alfred sat,
And sway'd the sceptre of his infant realms;
And such in ancient halls and mansions drear
May still be seen, but perforated sore
And drill'd in holes the solid oak is found,
By worms voracious eating through and through.

At length a generation more refined
Improv'd the simple plan, made three legs four,
Gave them a twisted form vermicular,
And o'er the seat with plenteous wadding stuff'd
Induced a splendid cover green and blue,
Yellow and red, or tap'stry richly wrought
And woven close, or needle-work sublime.
There might ye see the pioney spread wide,
The full-blown rose, the shepherd and his lass,
Lap-dog and lambkin with black staring eyes,

And parrots with twin cherries in their beak.

Now came the cane from India, smooth and bright
With Nature's varnish; sever'd into stripes
That interlaced each other, these supplied
Of texture firm a lattice work, that braced
The new machine, and it became a chair.
But restless was the chair; the back erect
Distress'd the weary loins that felt no ease;
The slipp'ry seat betray'd the sliding part
That press'd it, and the feet hung dangling down.
Anxious in vain to find the distant floor.
These for the rich: the rest, whom fate had placed
In modest mediocrity, content
With base materials, sat on well tann'd hides
Obdurate and unyielding, glassy smooth,
With here and there a tuft of crimson yarn,
Or scarlet crewel[11] in the cushion fixt:
If cushion might be call'd, what harder seemed
Than the firm oak of which the frame was form'd
No want of timber then was felt or fear'd
In Albion's happy isle. The lumber[12] stood
Ponderous and fixt by its own massy weight.
But elbows still were wanting; these, some say,
An Alderman of Cripplegate contrived,
And come ascribe th'invention to a priest
Burly and big and studious of his ease.
But rude at first, and not with easy slope
Receding wide, they press'd against the ribs,
And bruised the side, and elevated high,
Taught the rais'd shoulders to invade the ears.
Long time elapsed or e'er our rugged sires
Complain'd though incommodiously pent in,
And ill at ease behind. The Ladies first
'Gan murmur, as became the softer sex.
Ingenious fancy, never better pleas'd
Than when employ'd t'accommodate the fair,
Heard the sweet moan with pity, and devised
The soft settee; one elbow at each end;
And in the midst an elbow, it receiv'd
United yet divided, twain at once.
So sit two Kings of Brentford[13] on one throne;
And so two citizens who take the air,
Closed pack'd and smiling in a chaise and one.
But relaxation of the languid frame
By soft recumbency of outstretched limbs,

Was bliss reserved for happier days. So slow
The growth of what is excellent, so hard
T'attain perfection in this nether world.
Thus first necessity invented stools,
Convenience next suggested elbow chairs,
And luxury th'accomplish'd Sofa last.

William Cowper (1731–1800)

11 Crewel: fine worsted.

12 *Umber* 1785: *lumber* first 1800.

13 Characters in *The Rehearsal*, a play by John Sheffield, Duke of Buckingham. 'They were represented as
    entering the stage hand in hand, and sitting upon one throne.' – James Elroy Flecker (1884-1915)

99

On a Cornelian Heart
which was Broken (1812)

Ill-fated Heart! and can it be
That thou shouldst thus be rent in twain?
Have years of care for thine and thee
Alike been all employ'd in vain?

Yet precious seems each shatter'd part,
And every fragment dearer grown,
Since he who wears thee feels thou art
A fitter emblem of *his own*.

George Gordon,
Lord Byron (1788–1824)

100

On the Sale by Auction of Keats's Love-letters

These are the letters which Endymion wrote
To one he loved in secret, and apart.
And now the brawlers of the auction mart
Bargain and bid for each poor blotted note,
Ay! for each separate pulse of passion quote
The merchant's price. I think they love not art
Who break the crystal of a poet's heart
That small and sickly eyes may glare and gloat.

Is it not said that many years ago,
In a far Eastern town, some soldiers ran
With torches through the midnight, and began
To wrangle for mean raiment, and to throw
Dice far the garments of a wretched man,
Not knowing the God's wonder, of His woe?

Oscar Wilde (1856–1900)

101

A Virtuoso

Be seated, pray. 'A grave appeal'?
The sufferers by the war, of course;
Ah, what a sight for us who feel, –
This monstrous *melodrama* of Force!
We, Sir, we connoisseurs, should know,
On whom its heaviest burden falls;
Collections shattered at a blow,
Museums turned to hospitals!

'And worse,' you say; 'the wide distress!'
Alas, 'tis true distress exists,
Though, let me add, our worthy Press
Have no mean skill as colourists;
Speaking of colour, next your seat
There hangs a sketch from Vernet's hand;
Some Moscow fancy, incomplete,
Yet not indifferently planned;

Note specially the gray old Guard,
Who tears his tattered coat to wrap
A closer bandage round the scarred
And frozen comrade in his lap; –
But, as regards the present war, –
Now don't you think our pride of pence
Goes – may I say it? – somewhat far
For objects of benevolence?

You hesitate. For my part, I –
Though ranking Paris next to Rome,
Aesthetically – still reply
That 'Charity begins at Home.'
The words remind me. Did you catch
My so-named 'Hunt'? The girl's a gem;
And look how those lean rascals snatch
The pile of scraps she brings to them!

'But your appeal's for home,' – you say, –
For home, and English poor! Indeed!
I thought Philanthropy to-day
Was blinded to domestic need –
However sore – Yet though one grants
That home should have the foremost claims,
Assume intelligible names;

While here with us – Ah! who could hope
To verify the varied pleas,
Or from his private means to cope
With all our shrill necessities!
Impossible! One might as well
Attempt comparison of creeds;
Or fill that huge Malayan shell
With these half-dozen Indian beads.

And life is short, – I see you look
At yonder dish, a priceless bit;
You'll find it etched in Jacquemart's book,
They say that Raphael painted it; –
And life is short, you understand;
So, if I only hold you out
An open though an empty hand,
Why, you'll forgive me, I've no doubt.

Nay, do not rise. You seem amused;
One can but be consistent, Sir!
'Twas on these grounds I just refused
Some gushing lady-almoner, –
Believe me, on those very grounds.
Good-bye, then. Ah, a rarity!
That cost me quite three hundred pounds, –
That Dürer figure, – 'Charity'.

Austin Dobson (1840–1921)

102

Blue-dash Charger

Adam and Eve on a dish:
1680 or so: Bristol-made.
It hangs in the kitchen, a thing
We prize for its strangeness, age,
And maybe because it's rare.
It cost me a week's work.

With simple inherited skill,
No finesse but a crude delight,
Whoever painted its face
In green, yellow, blue and brown
Knew what the job in hand was.
He had a surface to fill.

Adam, in curly brown wig,
Round-bellied, long-buttocked, holds out
One hand: the other is raised
Perhaps in doubt, or perhaps
Simply to balance the stance
Of the woman who shares the design –

Eve, breasts scooped by the brush,
Who stands with her long coarse hair
Swathed round such innocent parts
As the craftsman wished to suggest.
An apple in either hand,
Like a doll she waits with him there.

A leaf as big as his head
Is slapped across Adam's groin.
The snake, with a bull-calf's face,
Squints sideways down at the sight,

Nudging one apple Eve holds
With a blunt blue muzzle. The tree,
Where he grows as the only branch,
Is solid down to the earth
But the earth itself is one blur
Of blue, wiped, sponged, a mere trail
Dragged up to the blue-dashed rim.
The biggest fruit lie at the top.

Ungainly, this work, and not
Even with much new to say.
Such stories survive like this dish,
Childishly-done, with a chip
That might ruin the whole effect
But doesn't. A pure ornament.

An object for one who collects
Objects, it covers a span
More than its surface, a truth,
A myth, or a spoiled man's whim,
Anonymous innocence stuck
In an attitude, on a wall.

Anthony Thwaite (1930–)

103

On the Portrait of a Scholar of the Italian Renaissance

The color, quick in fluid oil,
Affirms the flesh and lambent hair;
And darkness, in its fine recoil,
Confesses that the Mind is there.

With heavy lip, with massive curls,
With wisdom weighted, strong and dense,
The flesh is luminous as pearls;
The eyes ingenuous but intense.

The face is noble; but the name
Is one that we shall scarcely hold.
This is a vision in a frame,
Defined and matted down with gold.

Our names, with his, are but the lees
Residual from this clear intent;
Our finely grained identities
Are but this golden sidement.

Yvor Winters (1900–68)

104

Her China Cup

Her china cup is white and thin;
A thousand times her heart has been
Made merry at its scalloped brink;
And in the bottom, painted pink,
A dragon greets her with a grin.

The brim her kisses loves to win;
The handle is a manikin,
Who spies the foes that chip or chink
Her china cup.

Muse, tell me if it be a sin:
I watch her lift it past her chin
Up to the scarlet lips and drink
The Oolong draught, somehow I think
I'd like to be the dragon in
Her china cup.

Dempster Sherman (1860–1916)